THE BERKELEY SERIES IN AMERICAN HISTORY

Rebel versus Tory: The Crises of the Revolution, 1773-1776

Edited by

JACKSON T. MAIN

SAN JOSE STATE UNIVERSITY

RAND McNALLY & COMPANY · CHICAGO

The Berkeley Series in American History
Charles Sellers, editor

CONTENTS

INTRODUCTION

THE NAME OF TORY IS ODIOUS TO THE AMERICAN MIND. WE ARE PREJUDICED
by an apparent contrast between the patriotic heroes of the Revolution
and their traitorous enemies, for if, as we assume, the rebels defended
liberty, then the Tories must have subverted it. This impression is rein-
forced by the fact that the words of our Founding Fathers have been
preserved, published, assigned, and believed, whereas who has read the
protests of a Seabury or a Smith? Moreover, the conviction that the rebels
were right seems verified by their success. We are apt to judge morality
by the outcome, and when Cornwallis surrendered at Yorktown he acknowledged, so to speak, the superior virtue of the winners. The rebels
were right; the losers forever damned.

Now of course we know that victory proves nothing of the sort. We
cannot condemn the Tories as morally inferior, disloyal, or even wrong
merely because they lost and because their successful enemies said that
they were these things. The following selections will demonstrate that they
acted from principle and believed that they, not the rebels, were true de-
fenders of liberty. They may have been wrong: the reader can be the judge
of that.

Our purpose here, therefore, is in part to match the enemies once
again, to learn why they believed as they did, why some were loyal to
England, and others to a revolution. These writings, however, reveal far
more than the ideas of victors and vanquished: they actually helped to
decide the conflict. The people of America faced three great crises
between 1773 and 1776. As each crisis arose, there was a struggle for
supremacy between the "radicals," who advocated intense, even violent
resistance to England, and the "conservatives," who urged moderation and
peace. In between the two extremes most people hesitated. Upon their
choice depended the outcome, and at each crisis the radicals won. The
result was the Revolution: the radicals became rebels, the conservatives
(with many exceptions), Tories.

Why did the radicals win? There were many reasons, but one was that
at each crisis they succeeded in convincing people that they were correct

— that resistance was essential. During these years the newspapers and magazines were filled with the debate; in pamphlets, sermons, letters, speeches, and resolutions the battle was waged. There are times in history when such an argument means nothing, but in the Revolutionary era the victory of the radicals was achieved at least partly by their success in this debate. The selections below, therefore, not only reveal the reasons which men gave for their beliefs, but actually helped to form those beliefs. When we read the works of these authors we must ask not only what they had to say and how they differed, but why one succeeded and the other failed.

The first crisis came after the passage of the Tea Act. By that time the dispute between colonies and mother country had existed for some years, and many Americans had already taken decisive stands on the issues between them. The selections given in the first section introduce the different interpretations of the past conflicts and show how these were dividing Americans into radicals and conservatives. When the Tea Act was passed, the colonists had to decide whether to submit and peacefully protest, or resist, by force if necessary. The radicals succeeded in committing the colonists to resistance. Parliament responded with the "Intolerable" or "Coercive" Acts, and the second crisis began. Once more the radicals forced action by persuading a majority in the Continental Congress to adopt the Continental Association. Radical strength made this Association effective. Finally the last great crisis pitted Tory against Whig, Loyalist against rebel. Once again the radicals were victorious: conciliation was rejected, and independence declared.

In reading these selections we must first ask what immediately was at stake — what action is being urged or resisted? Second, what arguments are presented for and against the alternatives? Third, what is revealed concerning the ideas and attitudes of rebels and Tories: How did they differ? Is one to be preferred to the other? Finally, we must remember that on each occasion the radicals won the argument. Why did the rebels succeed?

I

THE BACKGROUND

THE FOLLOWING TWO ACCOUNTS TRACE THE COURSE OF EVENTS WHICH PRE-
ceded the first crisis and show how the colonials were already divided in
their opinions. It is especially instructive that interpretations so opposite
were expressed by men whose backgrounds were so similar. Both Francis
Hopkinson and Daniel Leonard were in their thirties. Both came of
wealthy families, were given college educations, and were lawyers. Both
were members of the Governor's Council and both became judges after the
war. Both were critical of the early British measures. But Leonard had a
long talk with Thomas Hutchinson, wrote the "Massachusettensis" series,
and became a Loyalist, while Hopkinson (after unsuccessfully seeking
political preferment in London) signed the Declaration of Independence
and designed the American flag. The student will of course note the differences between the ideas of the two men, but especially it is necessary to
ask why Hopkinson's point of view was more acceptable to most colonists
than was Leonard's.

In Hopkinson's story, the nobleman is of course the king, his wife,
Parliament, and the steward, the ministry. (*The miscellaneous essays and
occasional writings of Francis Hopkinson,* 3 vols. [Philadelphia, 1792], I,
65–85.)

A.

"A PRETTY STORY.
WRITTEN IN THE YEAR 1774."

Chap. I

ONCE UPON a time, a great while ago, there lived a certain nobleman,
who had long possessed a very valuable farm, and had a great number of
children and grand-children.

Besides the annual profits of his farm, which were very considerable,
he kept a large shop of goods; and being very successful in trade, he be-

came in process of time exceeding rich and powerful, insomuch that all his neighbours feared and respected him.

He had examined all the known systems of oeconomy, and selected from them, for the government of his own family, all such parts as appeared to be equitable and beneficial, and omitted those which experience had shown to be inconvenient or prejudicial: or rather, by blending their several constitutions together, he had so ingeniously counter-balanced the evils of one by the benefits of another, that the advantages were fully enjoyed, and the inconveniences scarcely felt.

He never exercised any undue authority over his children or servants; neither indeed could he greatly oppress them, if he was ever so disposed; for it was particularly covenanted in his marriage articles, that he should never impose any task or hardships upon his children without the consent of his wife.

Now the custom in his family was this: — that at the end of every seven years his marriage became null and void, at which time his children and grand-children met together and chose another wife for him, whom the old gentleman was obliged to marry under the same articles and restrictions as before. By this means the children had always a great interest in their mother-in-law, and through her a reasonable check upon their father's temper. For, besides that he could do nothing material respecting them without her approbation, she was sole mistress of the purse-strings, and gave him from time to time such sums as *she* thought necessary for expences of his family.

Being one day in a very extraordinary good humour, he gave his children a writing under hand and seal, by which he released them from many badges of dependence, and confirmed to them several very important privileges. The chief of these were, that none of his children should be punished for any offence, or supposed offence, until twelve of his brethren had examined the facts, and declared him subject to such punishment; and, secondly, he renewed his assurances that no tasks or hardships should be imposed upon them without the consent of their mother-in-law.

This writing, on account of its singular importance, was called THE GREAT PAPER. . . .

Chap. II

Now it came to pass, that this nobleman had, by some means or other, acquired a right to an immense tract of wild, uncultivated country, at a vast distance from his mansion-house. But he set little store by this estate, as it yielded him no profit, nor was it likely so to do; being not only difficult of access on account of the distance, but was inhabited by numerous wild beasts, very fierce and savage, so as to render it very dangerous to attempt taking possession of it.

In process of time, however, some of his children, more stout and enterprising than the rest, requested leave of their father to go and settle in this distant country. Leave was readily obtained: but before they set out, certain articles were stipulated between them. The old gentleman engaged on his part to protect the adventurers in their new settlement;

to assist them in chasing away the wild beasts; and to extend to them all the essential privileges and benefits of the government under which they were born: assuring them, that although they would be removed so far from his presence, they should always be considered as the children of his family. At the same time he gave each of them a bond* for the faithful performance of these promises; in which it was moreover covenanted, that they should have the privilege of making such rules and regulations for the good government of their respective families as they should find most convenient: provided only, that these rules and regulations should not be contradictory to, or inconsistent with, the general established orders of his household.

In return, he insisted that they, on their parts, should at all times acknowledge him to be their father; that they should not deal with others without his leave, but send to his shop for what they might want, and not sell the produce of their lands to any but those he should point out.

These preliminaries being duly adjusted, our adventurers bid adieu to the comforts and conveniences of their father's house. Many and great were the difficulties and dangers they encountered on the way; but many more, and much greater, on their arrival in the new country. There they found mountains covered with impervious forests, and plains steeped in stagnated waters — no friendly roof to shelter them from the roaring tempest — no fortress to protect them from surrounding dangers — many sunk under sickness and disease, and others fell a prey to the barbarous natives of the country.

They began, however, under all disadvantages to clear the land. The woods resound with the strokes of the ax — they drain the waters from the sedged morass, and pour the sun beams on the reeking soil. They are compelled to exert all the powers of industry and economy for bare subsistence; and, like their first parents, when driven from paradise, to earn their bread with the sweat of their brows. In this work they were frequently interrupted by the incursions of the savages, against whom they defended themselves with great magnanimity.

After some time, however, by their indefatigable perseverance they found themselves comfortably settled, and had the delightful prospect of fields waving with luxuriant harvests, and orchards, glowing with the fruits of their labour.

In the mean time they kept up a constant correspondence with their father's family; and provided, at a great expence, the means of procuring from his shop such goods and merchandizes as they wanted, for which they duly paid out of the produce of their lands, and the fruits of their industry.

Chap. III

Now the new settlers had adopted a mode of government in their several families similar to that to which they had been accustomed in their father's house: particularly in taking a new wife at the end of certain periods of time, without whose consent they could do nothing material

*Charters [Hopkinson's note].

in the conduct of their affairs. Under these circumstances, they thrived exceedingly, and became very numerous, living in great harmony with each other, and in constitutional obedience to their father's wife.

To protect them against the incursions of the barbarous natives, and the attacks of some of their neighbours, the old nobleman sent a number of his servants, but then he required that they should reimburse him for the trouble and expence he was at in furnishing this assistance; and this they cheerfully did, by applying from time to time to their respective wives for the necessary cash.

Thus did matters go on for a considerable time, to the mutual benefit of the old and new farms. But at last the nobleman's wife began to look with an avaricious eye towards the new settlers; saying to herself, if by the natural consequence of their friendly intercourse with us, and constitutional dependence on me our wealth and power are so much encreased, how much more would they accumulate, if I can persuade them, that all they possess belonged originally to me, and that I may, in right of my prerogative, demand of them such portions of their earning as I please. At the same time, being well aware of the promises and agreements her husband had made, and of the tenor and force of the *Great Paper*, she thought it best to proceed with great caution, and determined to gain her point, if possible, by subtile and imperceptible steps. . . .

Thus she gradually proceeded in her plan, imposing internal taxes on the new settlers, under various pretences, and receiving the fruits of their toil with both hands: moreover she persuaded her husband to send amongst them, from time to time, a number of the most lazy and worthless of his servants, under the specious pretext of defending them in their settlements; but, in fact, to rid his house of their company, not having employment for them at home: and more especially to be a watch and a check upon the people of the new farm. . . .

Chap. IV

As the old nobleman advanced in years, he neglected the affairs of his family; leaving them chiefly to the management of his steward. Now the steward had actually debauched his wife, and gained an entire ascendency over her. She no longer deliberated upon measures that might best promote the prosperity of the old farm or the new; but said and did whatever the steward put into her head. Nay, so entirely was she under his influence, that she could not utter even *aye* or *no* but as he directed her. . . .

Now the old lady and the steward had set themselves strenuously against the people of the new farm; and began to devise ways and means for their total and unconditional subjection. And to this end they prevailed on the nobleman to sign and edict against the new settlers; in which it was declared, that, as children, it was their duty to contribute towards supplying their father's table with provisions, and towards the support of the dignity of his family; for which purposes it was ordained, that all their spoons, knives and forks, plates, and porringers, should be marked* with a certain mark by officers he should appoint for the purpose; for which

*The Stamp Act [Hopkinson's note].

marking they should pay certain fees into his strong box; and it was ordained, that they should not, under severe penalties, presume to use any
spoon, knife, fork, plate or porringer before it had been so marked by the
officer, and the fees paid.

The inhabitants of the new farm began now to see that their father's
affections were alienated from them; and that their mother was but a base
mother-in-law, governed by their enemy the steward. They were thrown
into great confusion and distress by this discovery. They wrote the most
supplicating letters to their father; in which they acknowledged their
dependence upon him in terms of the most sincere affection and respect.
They reminded him of the difficulties and hardships they had suffered in
settling this new farm; and pointed out the great addition of wealth and
power his family had acquired by their improvement of an unprofitable
wilderness; and showed him that all the fruits of their labour must, by a
natural circulation, finally enrich his money-box. They mentioned, in
terms of humility, his promises and engagements to them when they left
home, and the bonds* he had given them; and held up in a strong point of
view, the solemnity and importance of the *Great Paper*. They acknowledged that he ought to be re-imbursed the expences he had incurred upon
their account; and that it was their duty to assist in supporting the dignity
of the family. All this they declared they were willing and ready to do;
but requested that they might do it in the manner pointed out by the
Great Paper; by applying to their respective wives for the keys of their
money-boxes, and furnishing him from thence: but earnestly prayed that
they might not be subjected to the caprice and tyranny of an avaricious
mother-in-law, whom they had never chosen, and of a steward, who was
their declared enemy.

Some of these letters were intercepted by the steward; others indeed
were delivered to the nobleman: but he was persuaded not only to treat
them with contempt, but to insist the more strenuously on the right his wife
claimed to mark the knives and forks, plates and porringers, of the new
settlers.

When the people of the new farm heard of all the ill success of their
letters, and understood how matters were conducted in their father's
family, they were exceedingly alarmed and distressed. They consulted
together on the situation of affairs, and determined that they would no
longer submit to the arbitrary impositions of their mother-in-law, and of
their enemy the steward; that they considered the new decree as a direct
violation of the *Great Paper;* and would not pay obedience to it, but
would sup their broth and eat their pudding as usual, without having their
spoons, knives and forks, plates or porringers, marked by the new officers.

The old nobleman and his wife, finding that the new decree could
not be established without actual force, and fearing the consequences of
an open contest, thought fit to annul the offensive edict, under the pretence of *mere expediency;** declaring and protesting, at the same time,
that he and his wife had an undoubted right to mark all the furniture of
the new settlers, if they pleased, from the silver tankard in the closet to
the chamber-pot under the bed: that, with respect to them, he was not

*Charters [Hopkinson's note]

[7]

bound by the shackles of the *Great Paper;* and in a word, that he and wife had, and ought to have, an uncontroled power over them, their lives, liberties, and property.

The people, however, took little notice of these pompous declarations. They were glad that the marking decree was annulled; and were in hopes that by degrees things would settle in their former course, and mutual affection be again restored.

Chap. V

In the mean time the new settlers encreased exceedingly, their dealings at their father's shop became proportionably enlarged, and their partiality for their brethren of the old farm was sincere and manifest. They suffered, indeed, some inconveniences from the *protectors* which had been stationed amongst them, who became very troublesome in their houses. They introduced riot and intemperance into their families, debauched their daughters, and derided the orders they had made for their own good government. Moreover, the old nobleman had, at different times, sent over to them a great number of thieves, murderers, and robbers, who did much mischief by practising those crimes for which they had been banished from the old farm. But they bore those evils with as much patience as could be expected; not chusing to trouble their old father with complaints, unless in cases of important necessity.

Now the steward began to hate the new settlers with exceeding great hatred, and determined to renew his attack upon their peace and happiness. He artfully insinuated to the nobleman and his foolish wife, that it was very mean, and unbecoming their greatness, to receive the contributions of the people of the new farm through the consent of their respective wives: that upon this footing they might some time or other refuse to comply with his requisitions, if they should take into their heads to think them oppressive and unreasonable; and that it was high time they should be compelled to acknowledge his unlimited power and his wife's *omnipotence,* which, if not enforced now, they would soon be able to resist, as they were daily encreasing in numbers and strength.

Another decree was, therefore, prepared and published, directing that the people of the new farm should pay a certain stipend upon particular goods,* which they were not allowed to purchase any where but at their father's shop; specifying that this imposition should not be laid as an advance upon the original price of these goods, but should be paid as a tax on their arrival in the new farm; for the express purpose of supporting the dignity of the nobleman's family, and for re-imbursing the expences he pretended to have been at on their account.

This new decree occasioned great uneasiness. The people saw plainly that the steward and their mother-in-law were determined to enslave and ruin them. They again consulted together, and wrote, as before, the most dutiful and persuasive letters to their father — but to no purpose — a deaf ear was turned against all their remonstrances, and their humble requests rejected with contempt.

*Declaratory Act [Hopkinson's note].
*Painter's colours, glass, &c. [Hopkinson's note].

Finding that this moderate and decent conduct brought them no relief, they had recourse to another expedient: they bound themselves to each other in a solemn engagement,† not to deal any more at their father's shop, until this unconstitutional decree should be repealed, which they one and all declared to be a direct violation of the *Great Paper*.

This agreement was so strictly observed, that in a few months the clerks and apprentices in the old gentleman's shop began to raise a terrible outcry. They declared, that their master's trade was declining exceedingly, and that his wife and steward would by their mischievous machinations ruin the whole farm. They sharpened their pens, and attacked the steward, and even the old lady herself, with great severity: insomuch, that it was thought proper to withdraw this attempt also, upon the rights and liberties of the new settlers. One part only of the decree was left still in force, viz. the tax upon *water-gruel*.*

Now there were certain men† in the old farm, who had obtained an exclusive right of selling *water-gruel*. Vast quantities of this gruel were vended amongst the new settlers, as they were extremely fond of it, and used it universally in their families. They did not, however, trouble themselves much about the tax on *water-gruel;* they were well pleased with the repeal of the other parts of the decree, and fond as they were of this gruel, they considered it as not absolutely necessary to the comfort of life, and determined to give up the use of it in their families, and so avoid the effects of that part of the decree.

The steward found his designs again frustrated: but was not discouraged by the disappointment. He devised another scheme, so artfully contrived, that he though himself sure of success. He sent for the persons who had the sole right of vending *water-gruel;* and after reminding them of the obligations they were under to the nobleman and his wife for the exclusive privilege they enjoyed, he requested that they would send sundry waggons laden with gruel to the new farm; promising that the accustomed duty which they paid for their exclusive right should be taken off from all the gruel they should so send amongst the new settlers; and that in case their cargoes should come to any damage, the loss should be made good to them out of his master's coffers.

The gruel-merchants readily consented to this proposal; considering that if their cargoes were sold, their profits would be very great; and if they failed, the steward was to pay the damage. On the other hand, the steward hoped that the new settlers would not be able to resist a temptation, thus thrown in their way, of purchasing their favourite gruel, to which they had been so long accustomed; and if they did use it, subject to the tax aforesaid, he would consider this as a voluntary acknowledgment that the nobleman and his wife had a right to lay upon them what impositions they pleased, and as a resignation of the privileges of the *Great Paper*.

But the new settlers were well aware of this decoy. They saw plainly that the gruel was not sent for their accommodation; and that if they

†Non-importation agreement [Hopkinson's note].
*Tea [Hopkinson's note].
†The India company [Hopkinson's note].

suffered any part of it to be sold amongst them, subject to the tax imposed by the new decree, it would be considered as a willing submission to the assumed omnipotence of their mother-in-law, and a precedent for future unlimited impositions. Some, therefore, would not permit the waggons to be unladen at all; but sent them back untouched to the gruel-merchants; and others suffered them to unload, but would not touch the dangerous commodity; so that it lay neglected about the roads and highways till it was quite spoiled. But one of the new settlers, whose name was JACK, either from a keener sense of the injuries intended, or from the necessity of his situation, which was such that he could not send back the gruel, because of a number of mercenaries* whom his father had stationed in his house to be a watch over him — he, I say, being almost driven to despair, stove† to pieces the casks of gruel which had been sent him, and utterly destroyed the whole cargo.

B.

MASSACHUSETTENSIS

❨Leonard's articles, signed "Massachusettensis," were headed "ADDRESSED to the Inhabitants of the Province of Massachusetts Bay, December 19, 1774." The most famous reply was by John Adams writing under the name "Novanglus." (*Novanglus, and Massachusettensis; or Political Essays, published in the years 1774 and 1775, on the principal points of controversy, between Great Britain and her colonies* [Boston, 1819], pp. 147–51. Paragraphing supplied.)❩

At the conclusion of the late war, Great Britain found that though she had humbled her enemies, and greatly enlarged her own empire, that the national debt amounted to almost one hundred and fifty millions, and that the annual expence of keeping her extended dominions in a state of defence, which good policy dictates no less in a time of peace than war, was increased in proportion to the new acquisitions. Heavy taxes and duties were already laid, not only upon the luxuries and conveniences, but even the necessaries of life in Great Britain and Ireland.

She knew that the colonies were as much benefitted by the conquests in the late war, as any part of the empire, and indeed more so, as their continental foes were subdued, and they might now extend their settlements not only to Canada, but even to the western ocean. — The greatest opening was given to agriculture, the natural livelihood of the country, that ever was known in the history of the world, and their trade was protected by the British navy. The revenue to the crown, from America, amounted to but little more than the charges of collecting it. She thought it as reasonable that the colonies should bear a part of the national burden, as that they should share in the national benefit.

For this purpose the stamp-act was passed. The colonies soon found

---

*Board of Commissioners [Hopkinson's note].
†Destruction of the tea at Boston [Hopkinson's note].

that the duties imposed by the stamp-act would be grievous, as they were laid upon custom-house papers, law proceedings, conveyancing, and indeed extended to almost all their internal trade and dealings. It was generally believed through the colonies, that this was a tax not only exceeding our proportion, but beyond our utmost ability to pay. This idea, united the colonies generally in opposing it.

At first we did not dream of denying the *authority* of parliament to tax us, much less to legislate for us. We had always considered ourselves, as a part of the British empire, and the parliament, as the supreme legislature of the whole. Acts of parliament for regulating our internal polity were familiar. We had paid postage agreeable to act of parliament, for establishing a post-office, duties imposed for regulating trade, and even for raising a revenue to the crown without questioning the right, though we closely adverted to the rate or quantum. We knew that in all those acts of government, the good of the whole had been consulted, and whenever through want of information any thing grievous had been ordained, we were sure of obtaining redress by a proper representation of it.

We were happy in our subordination; but in an evil hour, under the influence of some malignant planet, the design was formed of opposing the stamp-act, by a denial of the right of parliament to make it. The love of empire is so predominant in the human breast, that we rarely find an individual content with relinquishing a power that he is able to retain; never a body of men. Some few months after it was known that the stamp-act was passed, some resolves of the house of burgesses in Virginia, denying the right of parliament to tax the colonies, made their appearance. We read them with wonder; they savoured of independence; they flattered the human passions; the reasoning was specious; we wished it conclusive. The transition, to believing it so, was easy; and we, and almost all America, followed their example, in resolving that the parliament had no such right. It now became unpopular to suggest the contrary; his life would be in danger that asserted it. The newspapers were open to but one side of the question, and the inflammatory pieces that issued weekly from the press, worked up the populace to a fit temper to commit the outrages that ensued.

A non-importation was agreed upon, which alarmed the merchants and manufacturers in England. It was novel, and the people in England then supposed, that the love of liberty was so powerful in an American merchant, as to stifle his love of gain, and that the agreement would be religiously adhered to. It had been said, that several thousands were expended in England, to foment the disturbances there. However that may be, opposition to the ministry was then gaining ground, from circumstances, foreign to this. The ministry was changed, and the stamp-act repealed. The repealing statute passed, with difficulty however, through the house of peers, nearly forty noble lords protested against giving way to such an opposition, and foretold what has since literally come to pass in consequence of it.

When the statute was made, imposing duties upon glass, paper, India teas, &c. imported into the colonies, it was said, that this was another instance of taxation, for some of the duted commodities were necessaries, we had them not within ourselves, were prohibited from importing them from any place except Great Britain, were therefore obliged to import them from Great Britain, and consequently, were obliged to pay the duties. Accordingly newspaper publications, pamphlets, resolves, non-importation agreements, and the whole system of American opposition was again put in motion. We obtained a partial repeal of this statute, which took off the duties from all the articles except teas.

This was the lucky moment when to have closed the dispute. We might have made a safe and honorable retreat. We had gained much, perhaps more than we expected. If the parliament had passed an act declaratory of their right to tax us, our assemblies had resolved, ten times, that they had no such right. We could not complain of the three-penny duty on tea as burdensome, for a shilling which had been laid upon it, for the purpose of regulating trade, and therefore was allowed to be constitutional, was taken off; so that we were in fact gainers nine-pence in a pound by the new regulation. If the appropriation of the revenue, arising from this statute was disrelished, it was only our striking off one article of luxury from our manner of living, an article too, which if we may believe the resolves of most of the towns in this province, or rely on its collected wisdom in a resolve of the house of representatives, was to the last degree ruinous to health. It was futile to urge its being a precedent, . . . they had many for laying duties on commodities imported into the colonies. And beside we had great reason to believe that the remaining part of the statute would be repealed, as soon as the parliament should suppose it could be done with honor to themselves, as the incidental revenue arising from the former regulation, was four fold to the revenue arising from the latter. A claim of the right, could work no injury, so long as there was no grievous exercise of it, especially as we had protested against it, through the whole, and could not be said to have departed from our claims in the least. We might now upon good terms have dropped the dispute, and been happy in the affections of our mother country; but that is yet to come.

Party is inseperable from a free state. The several distributions of power, as they are limited by, so they create perpetual dissentions between each other, about their respective boundaries; but the greatest source is the competition of individuals for preferment in the state. Popularity is the ladder by which the partizans usually climb. Accordingly, the struggle is, who shall have the greatest share of it. Each party professes disinterested patriotism, though some cynical writers have ventured to assert, that self-love is the ruling passion of the whole.

There were two parties in this province of pretty long standing, known by the name of whig and tory, which at this time were not a little imbittered against one another. Men of abilities and acknowledged probity were on both sides. If the tories were suspected of pursuing their private interest through the medium of court favor, there was equal reason to suspect the whigs of pursuing their private interest by the means of popularity. Indeed some of them owed all their importance to it, and must in a little time have sunk into obscurity, had these turbulent commotions then subsided.

The tories and whigs took different routs [routes], as usual. The tories, were for closing the controversy with Great Britain, the whigs for continuing it; the tories were for restoring government in the province, which had become greatly relaxed by these convulsions, to its former tone; the whigs were averse to it; they even refused to revive a temporary riot act, which expired about this time. Perhaps they thought that mobs were a necessary ingredient in their system of opposition.

However, the whigs had great advantages in the unequal combat; their scheme flattered the people with the idea of independence; the tories' plan supposed a degree of subordination, which is rather an humiliating idea; besides there is a propensity in men to believe themselves injured and oppressed whenever they are told so. The ferment, raised in their minds in the time of the stamp-act, was not yet allayed, and the leaders of the whigs had gained the confidence of the people by their successes in their former struggles, so that they had nothing to do but to keep up the spirit among the people, and they were sure of commanding in this province.

It required some pains to prevent their minds settling into that calm, which is ordinarily the effect of a mild government; the whigs were sensible that there was no oppression that could be either seen or felt; if any thing was in reality amiss in government, it was its being too lax. So far was it from the innocent being in danger of suffering, that the most atrocious offenders escaped with impunity. They accordingly applied themselves to work upon the imagination, and to inflame the passions; for this work they possessed great talents; I will do justice to their ingenuity; they were intimately acquainted with the feelings of man, and knew all the avenues to the human heart. Effigies, paintings, and other imagery were exhibited; the fourteenth of August was celebrated annually as a festival in commemoration of a mob's destroying a building, owned by the late Lieutenant Governor, which was supposed to have been erected for a stamp-office; and compelling him to resign his office of stamp-master under liberty tree; annual orations were delivered in the old south meeting house, on the fifth of March, the day when some persons were unfortunately killed by a party of the twenty-ninth regiment; lists of imaginary grievances were continually published; the people were told weekly that the ministry had formed a plan to enslave them; that the duty upon tea was only a prelude to a window tax, hearth tax, land tax, and poll tax; and these were only paving the way for reducing the country to lordships. This last bait was the more easily swallowed, as there seems to be an apprehension of that kind hereditary to the people of New-England; and were conjured by the duty they owed themselves, their country, and their God, by the reverence due to the sacred memory of their ancestors, and all their toils and sufferings in this once inhospitable wilderness, and by their affections for unborn millions, to rouse and exert themselves in the common cause.

This perpetual incantation kept the people in continual alarm. We were further stimulated by being told, that the people of England were depraved, the parliament venal, and the ministry corrupt; nor were attempts wanting to traduce Majesty itself. The kingdom of Great Britain was depicted as an ancient structure, once the admiration of the world, now sliding from its base, and rushing to its fall. At the same time we were called upon to mark our own rapid growth, and behold the certain evidence that America was upon the eve of independent empire.

When we consider what effect a well written tragedy or novel has on the human passions, though we know it to be all fictitious, what effect must all this be supposed to have had upon those, that believed these high wrought images to be realities?

The tories have been censured for remissness in not having exerted themselves sufficiently at this period. The truth of the case is this; they saw and shuddered at the gathering storm, but durst not attempt to dispel it, lest it should burst on their own heads. Printers were threatened with the loss of their bread for publishing freely on the tory side. One Mr. Mein was forced to fly the country for persisting in it.

All our dissenting ministers were not inactive on this occasion. When the clergy engage in a political warfare, religion becomes a most powerful engine, either to support or overthrow the state. What effect must it have had upon the audience to hear the same sentiments and principles, which they had before read in a newspaper, delivered on Sundays from the sacred desk, with a religious awe, and the most solemn appeals to heaven, from lips which they had been taught, from their cradles, to believe could utter nothing but eternal truths? What was it natural to expect from a people bred under a free constitution, jealous of their liberty, credulous, even to a proverb, when told their privileges were in danger, thus wrought upon in the extreme? I answer, outrages disgraceful to humanity itself. What mischief was not an artful man, who had obtained the confidence and guidance of such an enraged multitude, capable of doing? He had only to point out this or the other man, as an enemy of his country; and no character, station, age, or merit could protect the proscribed from their fury. Happy was it for him, if he could secrete his person, and subject his property only to their lawless ravages. By such means, many people naturally brave and humane, have been wrought upon to commit such acts of private mischief and public violence, as will blacken many a page in the history of our country.

II

THE TEA CRISIS

THE FIRST CRISIS OF THE CLIMATIC SERIES BEGAN WHEN THE TEA ARRIVED. The act of Parliament had made the tea cheaper than before in spite of the tax, and the British government hoped that the colonials would therefore buy it, tax and all. No one on this side of the Atlantic approved of the measure, but many thought that obedience and remonstrance were more apt to obtain its repeal than actions which would antagonize England. The radicals' threats of violence and coercion against anyone opposing them only made the conservatives more alarmed at the consequences of resistance. The issues were made clear by a series of resolutions passed at town meetings and various unofficial gatherings. Most of these meetings were called by the radicals who seized the initiative. The crisis was a brief one, for the radicals settled the matter by returning, seizing, or destroying the tea. Although only a small number of people were involved directly, it is probable that a majority approved of these activities.

The different views are represented here by a statement of the New York City radicals and by a counterargument of Plymouth, Massachusetts, conservatives. Once again the general question is, what advantage did the radicals have in this debate? It will be noted that both sides claim to be defending the "liberties" or "true interests" of America. What were these liberties and interests, and who was more truly their defender?

A.

THE ASSOCIATION OF THE
SONS OF LIBERTY OF NEW YORK

❡ The "association" circulated and then enforced in New York City was similar to those in Philadelphia, Boston, and other towns. Probably the initiative was taken not by the gentlemen, merchants, and lawyers, but by the "other inhabitants," who then obtained many reluctant signatures. (Hezekiah Niles, ed., *Principles and Acts of the Revolution in America* . . . [New York, 1876], pp. 169–70. Paragraphing supplied.)]

To the Public

THE FOLLOWING association is signed by a great number of the principal gentlemen of the city, merchants, lawyers, and other inhabitants of all ranks, and it is still carried about the city, to give an opportunity to those who have not yet signed to unite with their fellow-citizens, to testify their abhorrence to the diabolical project of enslaving America.

The association of the Sons of Liberty of New York

It is essential to the freedom and security of a free people, that no taxes be imposed upon them but by their own consent, or their representatives. For "what property have they in that which another may, by right, take when he pleases to himself?" The former is the undoubted right of Englishmen, to secure which they expended millions and sacrificed the lives of thousands. And yet, to the astonishment of all the world, and the grief of America, the commons of Great Britain, after the repeal of the memorable and detestable stamp-act, reassumed the power of imposing taxes on the American colonies; and, insisting on it as a necessary badge of parliamentary supremacy, passed a bill, in the seventh year of his present majesty's reign, imposing duties on all glass, painters' colors, paper and teas, that should, after the 20th of November, 1767, be "imported from great Britain into any colony or plantation in America." — This bill, after the concurrence of the lords, obtained the royal assent. And thus they who, from time immemorial, have exercised the right of giving to, or withholding from the crown, their aids and subsidies, according to their *own free will and pleasure*, signified by their representatives in Parliament, do, by the act in question, deny us, their brethren in America, the enjoyment of the same right.

As this denial, and the execution of that act, involves our slavery, and would sap the foundation of our freedom, whereby we should become slaves to our brethren and fellow subjects, born to no greater stock of freedom than the Americans — the merchants and inhabitants of this city, in conjunction with the merchants and inhabitants of the ancient American colonies, entered into an agreement to decline a part of their commerce with Great Britain, until the above mentioned act should be totally repealed. This agreement operated so powerfully to the disadvantage of the manufacturers of England that many of them were unemployed. To appease their clamors, and to provide the subsistence for them, which the non-importation had deprived them of, the parliament, in 1770, repealed so much of the revenue act as imposed a duty on glass, painters' colors, and paper, and left the duty on tea, as *a test of the parliamentary right to tax us*.

The merchants of the cities of New York and Philadelphia, having strictly adhered to the agreement, so far as it is related to the importation of articles subject to an American duty, have convinced the ministry, that some other measures must be adopted to execute parliamentary supremacy over this country, and to remove the distress brought on the East India Company, by the ill policy of that act. Accordingly, to increase the temptation to the shippers of tea from England, an act of parliament passed the last session, which gives the whole duty on tea, the company were subject to pay, upon the importation of it into England, to the purchasers and exporters; and when the company have ten millions of pounds of tea, in their ware-houses exclusive of the quantity they may want to ship, they are allowed to export tea, discharged from the payment of that duty, with which they were before chargeable. In hopes of aid in the execution of this project, by the influence of the owners of the American ships, application was made by the company to the captains of those ships to take the tea on freight; but they virtuously rejected it. Still determined on the scheme, they have chartered ships to bring the tea to this country, which may be hourly expected, to make an important trial of our virtue. If they succeed in the sale of that tea, we shall have no property that we can call our own, and then we may bid adieu to American liberty.

Therefore, to prevent a calamity which, of all others, is the most to be dreaded — slavery, and its terrible concomitants — we, the subscribers, being influenced from a regard to liberty, and disposed to use all lawful endeavors in our power, to defeat the pernicious project, and to transmit to our posterity, those blessings of freedom which our ancestors have handed down to us; and to contribute to the support of the common liberties of America, which are in danger to be subverted, *do,* for those important purposes, agree to associate together, under the name and style of the *sons of New York*, and engage our honor to, and with each other faithfully to observe and perform the following *resolutions, viz.*

1st. *Resolved,* That whoever shall aid, or abet, or in any manner assist, in the introduction of tea, from any place whatsoever, into this colony, while it is subject, by a British act of parliament, to the payment of a duty, for the purpose of raising a revenue in America, he shall be deemed an enemy to the liberties of America.

2d. *Resolved,* That whoever shall be aiding, or assisting, in the landing, or carting of such tea, from any ship, or vessel, or shall hire any house, store-house, or cellar or any place whatsoever, to deposit the tea, subject to a duty as aforesaid, he shall be deemed an enemy to the liberties of America.

3d. *Resolved,* That whoever shall sell, or buy, or in any manner contribute to the sale, or purchase of tea, subject to a duty as aforesaid, or shall aid, or abet, in transporting such tea, by land or water, from this city, until the 7th George III. chap. 46, commonly called the revenue act, shall be totally and clearly repealed, he shall be deemed an enemy to the liberties of America.

4th. *Resolved,* That whether the duties on tea, imposed by this act, be paid in Great Britain or in America, our liberties are equally affected.

5th. *Resolved,* That whoever shall transgress any of these resolutions, we will not deal with, or employ, or have any connection with him.

B.

PROTEST OF INHABITANTS
OF PLYMOUTH, MASSACHUSETTS

❡ On December 7, 1773, the town of Plymouth, Massachusetts, unanimously passed a set of vigorous resolutions against the Tea Act. A week later, as violence threatened, some of the residents tried unsuccessfully to have the resolves reconsidered, and when they failed, published the following protest. (*Massachusetts Gazette, and the Boston Weekly News-Letter* [December 23, 1773].)]

THAT IT is not only our right but our duty frankly and freely to express our sentiments on every matter which essentially concerns the safety and welfare of our country, is a trust which we apprehend cannot be denied.

Therefore, We who are inhabitants of the town of Plymouth neither captivated by sounds and declamations, nor deceived by the cunning stratagems of men who under the specious masque of patriotism have attempted to delude an innocent and loyal people; But firmly and steadily fix'd and determin'd to defend our rights and privileges, and to endeavour to hand to our posterity the blessings of peace and good government which were procured by our fathers and transmitted to Us, — Having taken into serious consideration the dangerous and fatal consequences which may arise from the late resolves pass'd at a meeting of this town on the seventh day of this instant December; Fearing that they may bring upon us the vengeance of affronted Majesty and his insulted authority, We cannot answer it to our God and our consciences unless we protest against the proceedings of said meetings, and publish to the world that we were not instrumental in procuring those mischiefs which may naturally be expected from such conduct. — And we do by these presents solemnly protest against the whole of said resolves as being repugnant to our ideas of Liberty, law and reason. With the first of said resolves we will not concern ourselves further than to observe that we cannot see the necessity of this town's adopting similar measures with the citizens of Philadelphia.

The 2d. contains a censure upon a number of gentlemen (who are appointed consignees by the East-India company) which we cannot think either decent or just. Nor can we suppose that they have forfeited that protection to which good citizens are entitled, or exposed themselves to the indignation of good men.

To the 3d. and 4th. We say that we think it an affront to the common sense of mankind and to the dignity of the laws, to assert that such a meeting as was held in the town of *Boston* on the first of this instant December, was either lawful or regular: And further that the said meeting and the conduct and determination therein do not appear to us to be either necessary or laudable, or in any degree meriting the gratitude of those who wish Well to America: But in our opinion those who by constitutional and lawful means have endeavoured to hinder their proceedings and to prevent the bad effects thereof, have in this instance shewn themselves to be firm friends to the freedom and *true* interests of this Country.

To the fifth we must observe,

That we do not think ourselves bound either in duty or gratitude to acknowledge any obligations to the body who composed that meeting, nor to aid and support them in carrying their votes and resolves into execution, nor do we intend to hazard our lives and fortunes in their defence: But on the contrary We suppose it our indispensible duty (as the faithful and loyal subjects of his most gracious Majesty King GEORGE the third) to manifest our abhorrence and detestation of every measure which has a tendency to introduce anarchy, confusion, and disorder into the state, whether the same be proposed by Bodies of Men or by an individual.

In Witness of all which we set our hands at *Plymouth* the thirteenth day of December, A.D. 1773.

III

THE CRISIS
OF THE ASSOCIATION

THE SECOND CRISIS FOLLOWED THE PASSAGE OF THE "INTOLERABLE" ACTS, IN which Parliament severely punished Boston. The inhabitants of the city had resisted governors, customs officials, officers of the army and navy, Parliament, and the King, and had fomented sedition in Massachusetts and in other colonies as well. The Boston Tea Party was the last straw. The British government determined to teach colony and city a lesson and to frighten all colonials into obedience. Parliament therefore passed four acts which reduced the political liberties of the colony, increased British control over the courts, required that the army be quartered in private homes if necessary, and completely closed the port of Boston. The Bostonians called for aid, urging that they suffered in the common cause, and that the colonials must meet this challenge to their liberties.

One group of colonials, while deprecating the acts, felt that Boston deserved some punishment, and counseled moderation. Most of all, they feared that liberty would suffer more when some colonials coerced all the rest than when Parliament coerced a few. The contrary demand for aggressive resistence and total support of Boston is illustrated first by an address published in Philadelphia on June 1, 1774, and second by the Gloucester (Virginia) resolutions. (Peter Force, ed., *American Archives*, 4 series I, 377–79, 538–39.) These arguments were successful, for the Continental Congress adopted the "Continental Association," banning all commercial intercourse with Britain. Notice here the identification of radicalism with "liberty" and patriotism.

A.

TO ALL THE ENGLISH COLONIES
OF NORTH AMERICA

REMEMBER THE fable of the bundle of sticks given by the father to his sons; it could not be *broken* until it was *divided*. We must stand or fall together. For the *Boston* Port Act carries in its principle and effects the certain, if not the immediate destruction of all the liberties of *America*, the ruin of all our property, and greatly endangers the safety of our persons; its nature is so malignant, and its operations will be so fatal to our whole temporal happiness, that it cannot fail to awaken the attention of all *America*. The most deliberate wisdom, the steady counsel, and firm resolution of *America*, never was, and it is hardly conceivable, ever can be more necessary than in this dreadful crisis.

I don't pretend to be able to comprehend all the evils, or to point out half the consequences of that alarming statute; but a few that occur appear to me to deserve great consideration.

1st. The Legislative power, by which it was enacted, is founded in a direct violation of the most essential and fundamental principle of the *English* Constitution, viz: *that no* ENGLISHMAN *shall be bound by any law to which he has not consented.*

2d. The ordinary object of human laws, is either the attainment of some benefit, resulting therefrom, or the remedy of a mischief. But this is a mere statute of vengeance, wreaked on the *Bostonians*, for opposing the Parliamentary duty on tea, and is, therefore, a practical proof as well as dreadful sample of the disposition of the *British* Parliament to hurl mighty destruction against all who oppose their impositions, whenever it is in their power to cause their resentment to be felt.

3d. The interest ruined by this Act of Parliamentary vengeance is immense, 'tis the trade and navigation of an ancient metropolis of one of the richest and oldest Provinces of *English America*, whose dignity and merit is second to none on this Continent; whose inhabitants are almost wholly of *English* descent; whose affections for the *English* nation, and attachment to *Hanoverian* succession have been rapturously warm; whose patience and perseverance, whose expense of lives and treasure in commencing and extending the conquests and settlements of *English America*, all far exceed the utmost claim or boast of any other *English* Colony. But they oppose the Tea Duty, therefore their merits are forgotten, their honour is laid in the dust; their interest, obtained by long and painful industry to the amount of hundreds of thousands, is ruined; their traitors are cherished and encouraged, their humble and dutiful petitions are rejected, their claims of right, founded in nature, in the *English* Constitution, and in their Charter, under the sacred sanction of the public faith, are spurned out of sight with anger and contempt.

4th. The extent and operation of this baneful Act is mostly confined to the harbour of *Boston*, and its appendages, but its principle extends to every inch of *English America*. The *Bostonians* have as good a right to their harbour, their shipping, their wharfs and landing places, as they have to their houses, gardens, streets, commons, country seats, and plantations, and as good a right as the *Philadelphians* have to theirs, and, therefore, nothing can be more manifest than this, viz: That the same principle, the same power, that can seize on and wrest the one, can, with equal right and authority, seize on and wrest all the others out of the hands and use of their present proprietors, and, therefore, it follows by a consequence, which I dare say the *British* Parliament don't mean to deny, that if we presume to oppose any Act they may make, however oppressive and tyrannical we may deem it, or even to affront any peevish officer they may appoint over us, or without any of these, if they should even conceit we affront them, or if, without even such conceit, they should take it into their heads to exercise the absurd plenitude of their power over us, I say, in any of these cases, the same Parliamentary power which has deprived the *Bostonians* of their harbour, wharfs, landing places, &c., can, with equal authority, deprive any and every *English* Colony on the Continent of theirs, and accordingly send a sufficient force of ships and soldiers to stop every port in them, and put an end to all their navigation and trade; and not that only, but drive them all from their houses, streets, cities, and plantations. I appeal to the public if these are strained consequences, and if the power that can do the one cannot, with equal right, do all the rest.

5th. This fatal Act, as far as it relates to personal covenants and contracts, not only makes void all bills of lading, charter parties, &c., relating to vessels and cargoes destined to the port of *Boston*, and which may arrive there after the first day of *June* next; but the principle of this manifestly extends to all written contracts and covenants whatsoever, sealed or unsealed; to all deeds of lands, mortgages, indentures, covenants, bonds, bills, notes, receipts, &c., for there can be no doubt that the same power which is able to vacate, by sovereign authority, covenants and contracts relative to navigation made by private persons on reasonable and lawful considerations, can vacate also all covenants and contracts relating to inland affairs, so that if we should happen to disapprove of the Tea Duty, the *Boston* Port Act, or any other law the *British* Parliament may see fit to make, we may expect soon to be visited with a law from them, vacating all our deeds of lands, indentures of servants, bonds, &c., empowering all our servants to run away, and every rascal that pleases to enter on our estates and turn us out of our houses, &c.

6th. This dreadful extent of power is claimed by the *British* Parliament, on whom we have not the least check, and whose natural prejudices will ever induce them to oppress us — they are not of our appointment, they do not hope for our votes, or fear the loss of them at a future election; they have no natural affection for us; they don't feel for us; they never expect to see us, and therefore do not court our smiles, or dread meeting our angry countenances. When they vote away our money, they don't, at the same time, give that of their own and their best friends with it, but, on the contrary, they ease themselves and their friends of the whole burthen they lay on us, and, therefore, will always have strong inducements to make our burdens as heavy as possible that they may lighten their own. Indeed, in every view of this Act, it appears replete with horrour, ruin, and woe, to all *America;* it matters not where it begins to operate, no Colony on the Continent is exempt from its dreadful principle, nor can any one that has a seaport avoid its execution. But however ghostly, grinning, and death-like this awful threatening power lowers over us, I doubt not there are means left to *America* to avoid its effects, and virtue enough to induce every individual to throw aside every little consideration and unite with immoveable firmness in the important business of self-preservation.

We have reason to think this is the last effort of the power that would oppress us; if it takes place we are undone, undone with our posterity. If we oppose and avoid it, we may still continue to enjoy our liberties, and posterity will look back to this alarming period, and will admire and boast the virtue of their ancestors that saved them from slavery and ruin.

B.

RESOLVES OF THE INHABITANTS
OF GLOUCESTER COUNTY, VIRGINIA

AT A general and full Meeting of the Inhabitants of the County of *Gloucester*, at the Court House of the said County, after due notice, on *Thursday*, the 14th of *July*, 1774, JAMES HUBBARD, Esquire, Judge of the said County Court, being unanimously chosen *Moderator*,
They came to the following Resolves:

Resolved, That we will ever maintain and defend his Majesty's right and title to the Crown of *Great Britain*, and his Dominions in *America*, to whose royal person we profess the firmest attachment.

Resolved, That it is the opinion of this meeting, that taxation and representation are inseparable; and that as we are not, and, from the nature of things, cannot be, represented in the *British* Parliament, every attempt of that body to impose internal taxes on *America*, is arbitrary, unconstitutional, and oppressive.

Resolved, That the Act for blocking up the harbour of *Boston*, and other purposes therein mentioned, is cruel and unjust, and a convincing proof of the fixed intention of Parliament to deprive *America* of their constitutional rights and liberties.

Resolved, That the cause of *Boston* is the common cause of all *America*, and that we will firmly unite with the other counties in this Colony, and the other Colonies on this Continent, in every measure that may be thought necessary on this alarming occasion.

Resolved, That we do most heartily concur with our late Representatives in their resolve of the total disuse of tea, and do farther resolve against the use of any *East India* commodity whatsoever, except saltpetre.

Resolved, That we will not import, or purchase when imported, any merchandise or commodities from *Great Britain;* and that, at a short day hereafter to be fixed, we will stop all exports to *Great Britain*, until there is a total repeal of the *Boston* Port Act, all the several Acts imposing taxes on *America*, for the purpose of raising a revenue, and those other Acts made particularly against our brethren of the *Massachusetts Bay*, on account of their noble opposition to the late Revenue Acts.

Resolved, That should our sister Colonies of *Maryland* and *North Carolina* determine not to export their tobacco to *Great Britain*, we will be far from availing ourselves of their patriotic resolution, by continuing to export ours.

Resolved, That we will submit to any resolutions that may be entered into either by the Deputies of the several counties in this Colony at

Williamsburg, or by the general Congress of the Colonies on the Continent.

Resolved, That we will not deal with any person or persons in this county who will not sign this Association, and strictly and literally conform to every distinct article thereof; nor with any other person or persons who will not sign, and strictly conform, to the particular resolves of their respective counties, but will for ever despise and detest them as enemies to *American* liberty.

Resolved, That it is the opinion of this meeting, that immediately upon the non-exportation plan taking place, neither the gentlemen of the bar, nor any other person, ought to bring any suit for the recovery of any debt, or prosecute farther any suit already brought, during the continuance of these resolutions, it being utterly inconsistent with such scheme for any man to be compelled to pay without the means wherewith he may pay.

Resolved, That we do most cordially approve of the intended meeting of the late Burgesses on the first of *August* next, at *Williamsburg*, and do depute *Thomas Whiting*, and *Lewis Burwell*, Esquires, our late worthy Representatives, to consult with the Deputies of the several counties of this Colony, and to adopt such measures as are agreeable to the foregoing resolutions, hereby engaging, on our parts, to conform thereto, and to support the same to the utmost of our power.

Resolved, That the Clerk of this meeting transmit to the Printers of both Gazettes, copies of the above Resolves, with the request of the county to insert them in their papers.

JASPER CLAYTON, *Clerk*.

C.

LETTERS OF A
WESTCHESTER FARMER

❡A vigorous criticism of the Association was written by Samuel Seabury, posing as a "Westchester Farmer." Seabury was in reality a doctor and Episcopalian minister with degrees from Yale and Edinburgh. A Loyalist during the war, he later became the first Episcopalian bishop of America. Seabury's is probably the ablest presentation of the Tory view, and it reveals both the intellectual basis for loyalism and emotions behind the Tory mind. It may have had some effect, for Westchester County was a Loyalist stronghold; yet this pamphlet not only demonstrates the strengths of Seabury's position but also the weaknesses which prevented its success. As in the debate over the Tea Act, both sides identify themselves with a defense of liberty. In the light of Seabury's argument, is it accurate to say that the American Revolution was a victory for freedom? Why did this pamphlet, effective though it undoubtedly was, fail to persuade the colonials? (*Letters of a Westchester Farmer [1774-1775] by the Reverend Samuel Seabury [1729-1796] edited with an introductory essay by Clarence H. Vance* [White Plains, N.Y.: Publications of the Westchester County Historical Society, 1930], VIII, 43–62.)]

[25]

My Friends and Countrymen,

PERMIT ME to address you upon a subject, which, next to your eternal welfare in a future world, demands your most serious and dispassionate consideration. The American Colonies are unhappily involved in a scene of confusion and discord. The bands of civil society are broken; the authority of government weakened, and in some instances taken away: Individuals are deprived of their liberty; their property is frequently invaded by violence, and not a single Magistrate has had courage or virtue enough to interpose. From this distressed situation it was hoped, that the wisdom and prudence of the Congress lately assembled at Philadelphia, would have delivered us. The eyes of all men were turned to them. We ardently expected that some prudent scheme of accommodating our unhappy disputes with the Mother-Country, would have been adopted and pursued. But alas! they are broken up without even attempting it: they have taken no one step that tended to peace: they have gone on from bad to worse, and have either ignorantly misunderstood, carelessly neglected, or basely betrayed the interests of all the Colonies.

I shall in this, and some future publication, support this charge against the Congress, by incontestible facts: But my first business shall be to point out to you some of the consequences that will probably follow from the Non-importation, Non-exportation, and Non-consumption Agreements, which they have adopted, and which they have ordered to be enforced in the most arbitrary manner, and under the severest penalties. On this subject, I choose to address myself to You the *Farmers* of the Province of New-York, because I am most nearly connected with you, being one of your number, and having no interest in the country but in common with you; and also, because the interest of the farmers in general will be more sensibly affected, and more deeply injured by these agreements, than the interest of any other body of people on the continent. Another reason why I choose to address myself to you is, because the Farmers are of the greatest benefit to the state, of any people in it: They furnish food for the merchant, and mechanic; the raw materials for most manufacturers, the staple exports of the country, are the produce of their industry: be then convinced of your own importance, and think and act accordingly.

The Non-importation Agreement adopted by the Congress is to take place the first day of December next; after which no goods, wares, or merchandize, are to be imported from Great-Britain or Ireland; no East-India Tea from any part of the world; no molasses, syrups, paneles, coffee, or pimento, from our islands in the West-Indies; no wine from Madeira, or the Western-Islands; no foreign indigo.

The Non-Exportation Agreement is to take effect on the tenth day of September next; after which we are not to export, directly or indirectly, any merchandize or commodity whatsoever to Great-Britain, Ireland, or the West-Indies, except RICE to Europe, — unless the several acts and parts of acts of the British Parliament, referred to by the fourth article of Association, be repealed.

The Non-consumption Agreement is to be in force the first day of March next; after which we are not to purchase or use any East-

India Tea whatsoever; nor any goods, wares, or merchandize from Great-Britain or Ireland, imported after the first of December, nor molasses, &c. from the West-Indies; nor wine from Madeira, or the Western Islands, nor foreign indigo.

Let us now consider the probable consequences of these agreements, supposing they should take place, and be exactly adhered to. The first I shall mention is, clamours, discord, confusion, mobs, riots, insurrections, rebellions, in Great-Britain, Ireland, and the West-Indies. This consequence does not indeed immediately affect You, the Farmers of New-York; nor do I think it a probable one: But the Congress certainly intended it should happen in some degree, or to the effect they propose from these agreements cannot possibly take place. They intend to distress the manufacturers in Great-Britain, by depriving them of employment — to distress the inhabitants of Ireland, by depriving them of flax-seed, and of a vent for their linens, — to distress the West-India people, by with-holding provisions and lumber from them, and by stopping the market for their produce. And they hope, by these means, to force them all to join their clamours with ours, to get the acts complained of, repealed. This was the undoubted design of the Congress when these agreements were framed; and this is the avowed design of their warm supporters and partizans, in common conversation.

But where is the justice, where is the policy of this proceedure? The manufacturers of Great-Britain, the inhabitants of Ireland, and of the West-Indies, have done us no injury. They have been no ways instrumental in bringing our distresses upon us. Shall we then revenge ourselves upon them? Shall we endeavour to starve them into a compliance with our humours? Shall we, without any provocation, tempt or force them into riots and insurrections, which must be attended with the ruin of many — probably with the death of some of them? Shall we attempt to unsettle the whole British Government — to throw all into confusion, because our self-will is not complied with? Because the ill-projected, ill-conducted, abominable scheme of some of the colonists, to form a republican government independent of Great-Britain, cannot otherwise succeed? — Good God! can we look forward to the ruin, destruction, and desolation of the whole British Empire, without one relenting thought? Can we contemplate it with pleasure; and promote it with all our might and vigour, and at the same time call ourselves *his Majesty's most dutiful and loyal subjects?* Whatever the Gentlemen of the Congress may think of the matter, the spirit that dictated such a measure, was not the spirit of humanity.

Next let us consider the policy, or rather impolicy of this measure. Instead of conciliating, it will alienate the affections of the people of Great-Britain. Of friends it will make them our enemies; it will excite the resentment of the government at home against us; and their resentment will do us no good, but, on the contrary, much harm.

Can we think to threaten, and bully, and frighten the supreme government of the nation into a compliance with our demands? Can we expect to force a submission to our peevish and petulant humours, by exciting clamors and riots in England? We ought to know the temper and spirit, the power and strength of the nation better. A single campaign, should she exert her force, would ruin us effectually. But should she choose less violent means, she has it in her power to humble us without hurting herself. She might raise immense revenues, by laying duties in England, Ireland and the West-Indies, and we could have no remedy left; for this non-importation scheme cannot last forever. She can embarrass our trade in the Mediterranean with Spain, Holland &c. nor can we help ourselves; for whatever regulations she should make, would effectually be enforced, by the same Navy that she keeps in readiness to protect her own trade. . . .

[Moreover we will not succeed in this attempt, for the people of Great Britain, Ireland and the West-Indies will not be sufficiently distressed.] The first distress will fall on ourselves: it will be more severely felt by us, than by any part of all his Majesty's dominions; and it will affect us the longest. The fleets of Great-Britain command respect throughout the globe. Her influence extends to every part of the earth. Her manufactures are equal to any, superior to most in the world. Her wealth is great. Her people enterprizing, and persevering in their attempts to extend and enlarge and protect her trade. The total loss of our trade would be felt only for a time. Her merchants would turn their attention another way. New sources of trade and wealth would be opened: New schemes pursued. She would soon find a vent for all her manufactures in spite of all we could do. Our malice would hurt ourselves only. Should our schemes distress some branches of her trade, it could be only for a time; and there is ability and humanity enough in the nation to relieve those that are distressed by us, and to put them in some other way of getting their living.

The case is very different with *us*. We have no trade but under the protection of Great-Britain. We can trade no where but where she pleases. We have no influence abroad, no ambassadors, no consuls, no fleet to protect our ships in passing the seas, nor our merchants and people in foreign countries. Should our mad schemes take place, our sailors, ship-carpenters, carmen, sail-makers, riggers, miners, smelters, forge-men, and workers in bar-iron, &c. would be immediately out of employ; and we should have twenty mobs and riots in our own country, before one would happen in Britain or Ireland. Want of food will make these people mad, and they will come in troops upon our farms, and take that by force which they have not money to purchase. And who could blame them? Justice, indeed, might hang them; but the sympathetic eye would drop the tear of humanity on their grave.

The next thing I shall take notice of, is the advanced prices of goods, which will, not only probably, but necessarily, follow, as soon as the non-importation from Great Britain, &c. shall take effect. This is a consequence that most nearly concerns you; nor can you prevent it. You are obliged to buy many articles of clothing. You cannot make them yourselves; or you cannot make them so cheap as you can buy them. You want Woollens for your winter clothing. Few of you have wool enough to answer the purpose. For notwithstanding the boasts of some ignorant, hot-headed men, there is not wool enough on the continent, taking all the colonies together, to supply the inhabitants with stockings. Notwithstanding all the home-spun you can make, many of you find it difficult, at the year's end, to pay the shop-keeper for what the necessities of your families have obliged you to take up. What will you do when the prices of goods are advanced a quarter, for instance, or an half? To say that the prices of goods will not be raised, betrays your ignorance and folly. The price of any commodity always rises in proportion to the demand for it; and the demand always increases in proportion to its scarcity. As soon as the importation ceases in New-York, the quantity of goods will be daily lessened, by daily consumption; and the prices will gradually rise in proportion. "But the merchants of New-York have declared that, they will demand only a reasonable profit." Who is to judge what a reasonable profit is? Why, the merchants. Will they expose their invoices, and the secrets of their trade to you, that you may judge whether their profits are reasonable or not? Certainly they will not, and if they did, you cannot understand them; and consequently, can form no judgment about them. You have therefore nothing to trust to in this case but the honour of the merchants. Let us then consider how far we have reason to trust to their honour.

Not to raise the price of a commodity when it is scarce, and in demand, is contrary to the principles and practice of merchants. Their maxim is, to buy as cheap, and sell as dear, as they can. Will they let you have a piece of goods for twenty shillings, which will fetch twenty-five? When the stores and shops are full, and a price is demanded which you think unreasonable, you will ask an abatement. If you are refused, you will look elsewhere. But when there are few goods and many buyers, no abatement can be expected. If you won't give the price, your neighbor perhaps is in greater necessity, and *must* give it. Besides, the merchant knows that no more goods can be imported. He knows that the necessities of the country are increasing, and that what you refuse now at twenty shillings, you will be obliged to take, by and by, at twenty-five. . . .

I come now to the consideration of another probable consequence of a Non-importation agreement, which is, That it will excite the resentment of the government at home against us, and induce the Parliament to block up our ports and prevent our trade intirely. It would certainly be good policy in the government to do so. Few Colonies are settled but by a trading people, and by them chiefly for the benefit of trade. The grand design of England in settling the American Colonies, was to extend her trade — to open a new vent for her manufacturers. If then we stop our imports, the benefit of our trade is in a manner lost to her, and she would find but little additional disadvantage, should she stop our trade with all the world.

But should the government pursue milder measures — though we indeed have no right to expect it will—yet the Congress have determined the expediency of our stopping our own trade, after a limited time, viz. ten months. In either case the consequence will be much the same; and it matters but little whether the government blocks up our ports, or whether we ourselves voluntarily put an end to our exports, as well as imports; after the 10th of September next we are to have but little trade except with our neighbouring colonies.

Consider the consequence, Should the government interpose, we shall have no trade at all, and consequently no vent for the produce of our farms. Such part of our wheat, flaxseed, corn, beef, pork, butter, cheese, as was not consumed in the province, must be left to rot and stink upon our hands.

Should the government leave us to ourselves, the little trade that would be open, would never keep these articles at such a price, as to make it worth while to raise more of them than we want for our own consumption.

Look well to yourselves, I beseech you. From the day that the exports from this province are stopped, the farmers may date the commencement of their ruin. Can you live without money? Will the shop-keeper *give* you his goods? Will the weaver, shoemaker, blacksmith, carpenter, work for you without pay? If they will, it is far more than they will do for me. And unless you can sell your produce, how are you to get money? Nor will the case be better, if you are obliged to sell your produce at an under-rate; for then it will not pay you for the labour and expence of raising it. But this is the least part of the distress that will come upon you.

Unhappily, many of you are in debt, and obliged to pay the enormous interest of seven pounds on the hundred, for considerable sums. It matters not whether your debts have been contracted through necessity, or carelessness: You must pay them, at *least* the interest, punctually; the usurer will not wait long; indeed you cannot expect he should: You have had his money, and are obliged, in justice, to pay him the principal and interest, according to agreement. But without selling your produce, you can neither pay the one, nor the other; the consequence will be that after a while, a process of law will be commenced against you, and your farms must be sold by execution; and then you will have to pay not only principal and interest, but Sheriffs fees, Lawyers fees, and a long list of *et caeteras*.

Nor, under these circumstances, will your farms fetch half what they cost you. What is a farm good for, the produce of which cannot be sold? Had matters continued in their old course, some one of your neighbours, who knew the value of your farm, might have been willing and able to have given you a reasonable price for it, had you been disposed, or obliged to sell; but he has more wit than to buy a farm, when he cannot sell its produce. Your creditor, then, or some rich merchant, or usurer, must take it at their own price: To you it is of no consequence who takes it; for you are ruined, stripped of your farm, and very probably of the means of subsistance for yourself and family. Glorious effect of Non-exportation! Think a little, and then tell me — when the Congress adopted this cursed scheme, did they in the least consider your interest? No, impossible! they ignorantly misunderstood, carelessly neglected, or basely betrayed you. . . .

Rouse, my friends, rouse from your stupid lethargy. Mark the men who shall dare to impede the course of justice. Brand them as the infamous betrayers of the rights of their country. The grand security of the property, the liberty, the lives of Englishmen, consists of the due administration of justice. While the courts are duly attended to, and fairly conducted, our property is safe. As soon as they are shut, everything is precarious: for neither property, nor liberty, have any foundation to stand upon.

Tell me not of Delegates, Congresses, Committees, Riots, Mobs, Insurrections, Associations, — a plague on them all. — Give me the steady, uniform, unbiassed influence of the Courts of Justice. I have been happy under their protection, and I trust in God, I shall be so again.

But after all, some of you, I fear, look forward with pleasure to those halcyon days of security, when the Courts shall be shut. Undisturbed by the clamours of creditors, undismayed by the sight of the Sheriff, you think to pass your lives in quietness and peace. — But ah! my friends! trust not the fatal, the ill-judged security. You would not, I hope, be so dishonest as not to do your utmost endeavor to pay your debts; besides, while the Courts of Justice are shut, you will be apt to be careless. You will neglect paying your interest, your debts will accumulate, your creditors will be irritated; and as soon as a legal process can be commenced, you will be ruined before you can look about you.

Some of you are indebted to the loan-office. You have your money, it is true, at a low rate: You pay only five *per centum:* But if you cannot sell your produce, you can no more pay five *per cent.* than seven. The shutting up of the Courts of Justice can here give you no relief. By virtue of the act which regulates the Loan-Office, your farms, if you fail to pay the interest, will be sold in a limited time, without any judicial process at all.

Some of you, also, are tenants at will; and if you fail in paying your rents, you may be turned off, with little or no warning.

Consider now the situation you will be in, if Great-Britain, provoked by your Non-Importation Agreement, should shut up our ports; or should the Non-Exportation agreed to by the Congress, take effect. In that case you will not be able to sell your produce: you cannot pay even the interest of the money you are indebted for; your farms must be sold, and you and your families turned out, to beggary and wretchedness. Blessed fruits of Non-Importation and Non-Exportation! The farmer that is in debt, will be ruined: the farmer that is clear in the world, will be obliged to run in debt, to support his family: and while the proud merchant, and the forsworn smuggler, riot in their ill-gotten wealth; the laborious farmers, the grand support of every well-regulated country, must go to the dogs together. — Vile! Shamefull! Diabolical Device!

Let us now attend a little to the Non-Consumption Agreement, which the Congress, in their Association, have imposed upon us. After the first of March we are not to purchase or use any East-India Tea whatsoever; nor any goods, wares, or merchandize from Great-Britain or Ireland, imported after the first day of December next: nor any molasses, syrups, &c. from the British plantations in the West-Indies, or from Dominica; nor wine from Madeira, or the Western Islands; nor foreign indigo.

Will you submit to this slavish regulation? — You must. — Our sovereign Lords and Masters, the High and Mighty Delegates, in Grand Continental Congress assembled, have ordered and directed it. They have directed the Committees in the respective colonies, to establish such further regulations as they may think proper, for carrying their association, of which this Non-consumption agreement is a part, into execution. Mr. **** *** of New-York, under the authority of their High-Mightinesses, the Delegates, by, and with the advice of his Privy Council, the Committee of New-York, hath issued his mandate, bearing date Nov. 7, 1774, recommending it to the freeholders and freemen of New-York, to assemble on the 18th of November, to choose eight persons out of every ward, to be a Committee, to carry the Association of the Congress into execution. — The business of the Committee so chosen is to be, to inspect the conduct of the inhabitants, and see whether they violate the Association. — Among other things, Whether they drink any Tea or wine in their families, after the first of March, or wear any British or Irish manufactures; or use any English molasses, &c. imported after the first day of December next. If they do, their names are to be published in the Gazette, that they might be *publickly known*, and *universally contemned*, as *foes to the Rights of British America, and enemies of American Liberty.* — And then *the parties of the said Association will respectively break off all dealings with him or her.* — In plain English, — They shall be considered as Out-laws, unworthy of the protection of civil society, and delivered over to the vengeance of a lawless, outrageous mob, to be *tarred, feathered, hanged, drawn, quartered, and burnt.* — O rare American Freedom!

Probably, as soon as this point is settled in New-York, the said Mr. **** *** in the plenitude of his power, by, and with the advice of his Privy Council aforesaid, will issue his Mandate to the supervisors in the several counties, as he did about the choice of Delegates, and direct them to have Committees chosen in their respective districts, for the same laudable purpose.

Will you be instrumental in bringing the most abject slavery on yourselves? Will you choose such Committees? Will you submit to them, should they be chosen by the weak, foolish, turbulent part of the country people? — Do as you please: but, by HIM that made me, I will not. — No, if I must be enslaved, let it be by a KING at least, and not by a parcel of upstart lawless Committee-men. If I must be devoured, let me be devoured by the jaws of a lion, and not *gnawed* to death by rats and vermin.

Did you choose your supervisors for the purpose of inslaving you? What right have they to fix up advertisements to call you together, for a very different purpose from that for which they were elected? Are our supervisors our masters? — And should half a dozen foolish people meet together again, in consequence of their advertisements, and choose themselves to be a Committee, as they did in many districts, in the affair of choosing Delegates, are we obliged to submit to such a Committee? —

You ought, my friends, to assert your own freedom. Should such another attempt be made upon you, assemble yourselves together: tell your supervisor, that he has exceeded his commission — That you will have no such Committees: — That you are Englishmen, and will maintain your rights and privileges, and will eat, and drink, and wear, whatever the public laws of your country permit, without asking leave of any illegal, tyrannical Congress or Committee on earth.

But however, as I said before, do as you please: If you like it better, choose your Committee, or suffer it to be chosen by half a dozen Fools in your neighbourhood, — open your doors to them, — let them examine your tea-cannisters, and molasses-jugs, and your wives and daughters petty-coats, — bow, and cringe, and tremble, and quake, — fall down and worship our sovereign Lord and Mob. — But I repeat it, By H — n, I will not. — No, my house is my castle: as such I will consider it, as such I will defend it, while I have breath. No *King's* officer shall enter it without my permission, unless supported by a warrant from a magistrate. — And shall my house be entered, and my mode of living enquired into, by a domineering Committeeman? Before *I* submit, I will die: live *you*, and be slaves.

D.

TO THE PRINTERS OF THE BOSTON NEWSPAPERS

⟨After Congress adopted the Association, local committees were organized to enforce it. Since those who, like Seabury, opposed the measure naturally refused to serve, these committees were controlled by the radical elements in each community. They tried to make everyone sign the Association, published the names of those who refused as enemies to their country, and saw to it that the agreement was obeyed, by force if necessary, though usually threats were sufficient. At this point, therefore, the colonial could no longer hesitate but must declare himself, one way or the other; and if he chose not to sign, his property and even his person might suffer. If the British government threatened his liberty from one side, fellow colonists threatened it from another. As an alternative to the Continental Association, Timothy Ruggles offered one of his own. A Harvard graduate, lawyer, judge, and country gentleman, Brigadier General Ruggles was not about to be intimidated, but even when this article was published he had been obliged to take refuge in army-occupied Boston. The radicals had won again.

What "rights" upheld by Ruggles were threatened by radical action? (Force, *American Archives*, 4 series I, 1057–58.)]

To the Printers of the Boston Newspapers

As MESSRS. *Edes* and *Gill*, in their paper of *Monday*, the 12th instant, were pleased to acquaint the publick, "that the Association sent by Brigadier *Ruggles*, &c., to the Town of *Hardwick*, &c., together with his son's certificate thereof, and the Resolves of the Provincial Congress thereon, must be referred till their next," I was so credulous as to expect then to have seen their next paper adorned with the form of an Association, which would have done honour to it, and, if attended to and complied with by the good people of the Province, might have put it in the power of any one very easily to have distinguished such loyal subjects to the King, as dare to assert their rights to freedom, in all respects consistent with the laws of the land, from such rebellious ones, under the pretext of being friends to liberty, are frequently committing the most enormous outrages upon the persons and properties of such of his Majesty's peaceable subjects, who, for want of knowing who to call upon (in these distracted times) for assistance, fall into the hands of a banditti, whose cruelties surpass those of savages; but finding my mistake, now take the liberty to send copies to your several offices to be published in your next papers, that so the publick may be made more acquainted therewith than at present, and be induced to associate for the above purposes; and as many of the people, for some time past, have been arming themselves, it may not be amiss to inform them that their numbers will not appear so large in the field as was imagined, before it was known that independency was the object in contemplation; since which many have associated in different parts of the Province to preserve their freedom and support Government; and as it may become necessary in a very short time to give convincing proofs of our attachment to Government, we shall be much wanting to ourselves if we longer trample upon that patience which has already endured to long-suffering, and may, if this opportunity be neglected, have a tendency to ripen many for destruction who have not been guilty of an overt act of rebellion, which would be an event diametrically opposite to the humane and benevolent intention of him whose abused patience cannot endure for ever, and who hath already, by his prudent conduct, evinced the most tender regard for a deluded people.

TIM. RUGGLES

The Association

We, the subscribers, being fully sensible of the blessings of good Government, on the one hand, and convinced, on the other hand, of the evils and calamities attending on tyranny in all shapes, whether exercised by one or many, and having of late seen, with great grief and concern, the distressing efforts of a dissolution of all Government, whereby our lives, liberties, and properties are rendered precarious, and no longer under the protection of the law; and apprehending it to be our indispensable duty to use all lawful means in our power for the defence of our persons and property against all riotous and lawless violence, and to recover and secure the advantages which we are entitled to from the good and wholesome laws of the Government, do hereby associate and mutually covenant and engage to and with each other as follows, namely:

1st. That we will, upon all occasions, with our lives and fortunes, stand by and assist each other in the defence of his life, liberty, and property, whenever the same shall be attacked or endangered by any bodies of men, riotously assembled, upon any pretence, or under any authority not warranted by the laws of the land.

2d. That we will, upon all occasions, mutually support each other in the free exercise and enjoyment of our undoubted right to liberty, in eating, drinking, buying, selling, communing, and acting what, with whom, and as we please, consistent with the laws of *God* and the King.

3d. That we will not acknowledge or submit to the pretended authority of any Congress, Committees of Correspondence, or any other unconstitutional assemblies of men; but will, at the risk of our lives, if need be, oppose the forcible exercise of all such authority.

4thly. That we will, to the utmost of our power, promote, encourage, and when called to it, enforce obedience to the rightful authority of our most gracious Sovereign, King *George* the Third, and of his laws.

5thly. That when the person or property of any of us shall be invaded or threatened by any Committees, mobs, or unlawful assemblies, the others of us will, upon notice received, forthwith repair, properly armed, to the person on whom, or the place where such invasion or threatening shall be, and will, to the utmost of our power, defend such person and his property, and, if need be, will oppose and repel force with force.

6thly. That if any one of us shall unjustly and unlawfully be injured, in his person or property, by any such assemblies as before mentioned, the others of us will unitedly demand, and, if in our power, compel the offenders, if known, to make full reparation and satisfaction for such injury; and if all our means of security fail, we will have recourse to the natural law of retaliation.

In witness of all which we hereto subscribe our names this ***** day of *****.

THE CRISIS

OF INDEPENDENCE

THE FINAL CRISIS WAS THE DEBATE OVER INEPENDENCE. IT BEGAN WHEN
Parliament adopted a plan of conciliation and when subsequently commissioners were appointed to negotiate a settlement. The British government offered to refrain from taxing any colony which promised to
furnish money for the army and for the royal administration generally.
This fell far short of the colonists' demands, but conservatives welcomed
the opportunity to negotiate and sought to delay any action which
might endanger a reunion. On the other hand some radicals now had
abandoned all hope of reconciliation. The majority of colonists hesitated, however, to take the final, irrevocable step. The debate over independence had already been raging for some weeks when there appeared
the most stirring polemic of the age: Thomas Paine's "Common Sense."
(Moncure Daniel Conway, *The Writings of Thomas Paine*, 4 vols. [New
York: Putnam, 1894–96], I, 84–101.)

Why was this pamphlet so exceptionally — perhaps decisively —
effective?

A.

COMMON SENSE

IN THE following pages I offer nothing more than simple facts, plain
arguments, and common sense: and have no other preliminaries to settle
with the reader, than that he will divest himself of prejudice and pre-
possession, and suffer his reason and his feelings to determine for themselves: that he will put on, or rather that he will not put off, the true
character of a man, and generously enlarge his views beyond the present day.

Volumes have been written on the subject of the struggle between
England and America. Men of all ranks have embarked in the controversy, from different motives, and with various designs; but all have
been ineffectual, and the period of debate is closed. Arms as the last

resource decide the contest; the appeal was the choice of the King, and the Continent has accepted the challenge.

It hath been reported of the late Mr. Pelham (who tho' an able minister was not without his faults) that on his being attacked in the House of Commons on the score that his measures were only of a temporary kind, replied, "*They will last my time.*" Should a thought so fatal and unmanly possess the Colonies in the present contest, the name of ancestors will be remembered by future generations with detestation.

The Sun never shined on a cause of greater worth. 'Tis not the affair of a City, a County, a Province, or a Kingdom; but of a Continent — of at least one-eighth part of the habitable Globe. 'Tis not the concern of a day, a year, or an age; posterity are virtually involved in the contest, and will be more or less affected even to the end of time, by the proceedings now. Now is the seed-time of Continental union, faith and honour. The least fracture now will be like a name engraved with the point of a pin on the tender rind of a young oak; the wound would enlarge with the tree, and posterity read it in full grown characters.

By referring the matter from argument to arms, a new era for politics is struck — a new method of thinking hath arisen. All plans, proposals, &c. prior to the nineteenth of April, *i.e.* to the commencement of hostilities, are like the almanacks of the last year; which tho' proper then, are superceded and useless now. Whatever was advanced by the advocates on either side of the question then, terminated in one and the same point, viz. a union with Great Britain; the only difference between the parties was the method of effecting it; the one proposing force, and other friendship; but it hath so far happened that the first hath failed, and the second hath withdrawn her influence.

As much hath been said of the advantages of reconciliation, which, like an agreeable dream, hath passed away and left us as we were, it is but right that we should examine the contrary side of the argument, and enquire into some of the many material injuries which these Colonies sustain, and always will sustain, by being connected with and dependant on Great-Britain. To examine that connection and dependance, on the principles of nature and common sense, to see what we have to trust to, if separated, and what we are to expect, if dependant.

I have heard it asserted by some, that as America has flourished under her former connection with Great-Britain, the same connection is necessary towards her future happiness, and will always have the same effect. Nothing can be more fallacious than this kind of argument. We may as well assert that because a child has thrived upon milk, that it is never to have meat, or that the first twenty years of our lives is to become a precedent for the next twenty. But even this is admitting more than is true; for I answer roundly that America would have flourished as much, and probably much more, had no European power taken any notice of her. The commerce by which she hath enriched herself are the necessaries of life, and will always have a market while eating is the custom of Europe.

But she has protected us, say some. That she hath engrossed us is true, and defended the Continent at our expense as well as her own is admitted; and she would have defended Turkey from the same motive, *viz.* for the sake of trade and dominion.

Alas! we have been long led away by ancient prejudices and made large sacrifices to superstition. We have boasted the protection of Great Britain, without considering, that her motive was *interest,* not *attachment;* and that she did not protect us from *our enemies* on *our account,* but from *her enemies* on *her own account,* and who will always be our enemies on the *same account.* Let Britain waive her pretensions to the Continent, or the Continent throw off the dependance, and we should be at peace with France and Spain, were they at war with Britain. The miseries of Hanover['s] last war ought to warn us against connections.

It hath lately been asserted in parliament, that the Colonies have no relation to each other but through the Parent Country, *i.e.* that Pennsylvania and the Jerseys, and so on for the rest, are sister Colonies by the way of England; this is certainly a very roundabout way of proving relationship, but it is the nearest and only true way of proving enmity (or enemyship, if I may so call it). France and Spain never were, nor perhaps ever will be, our enemies as *Americans,* but as our being the *subjects of Great Britain.*

But Britain is the parent country, say some. Then the more shame upon her conduct. Even brutes do not devour their young, nor savages make war upon their families; Wherefore, the assertion, if true, turns to her reproach; but it happens not to be true, or only partly so, and the phrase *parent* or *mother country* hath been jesuitically adopted by the King and his parasites, with a low papistical design of gaining an unfair bias on the credulous weakness of our minds. Europe, and not England, is the parent country of America. This new World hath been the asylum for the persecuted lovers of civil and religious liberty from *every part* of Europe. Hither have they fled, not from the tender embraces of the mother, but from the cruelty of the monster; and it is so far true of England, that the same tyranny which drove the first emigrants from home pursues their descendants still.

In this extensive quarter of the globe, we forget the narrow limits of three hundred and sixty miles (the extent of England) and carry our friendship on a larger scale; we claim brotherhood with every European Christian, and triumph in the generosity of the sentiment.

It is pleasant to observe by what regular gradations we surmount the force of local prejudices, as we enlarge our acquaintance with the World. A man born in any town in England divided into parishes, will naturally associate most with his fellow parishioners (because their interests in many cases will be common) and distinguish him by the name of *neighbor;* if he meet him but a few miles from home, he drops the narrow idea of a street, and salutes him by the name of *townsman;* if he travel out of the county and meet him in any other, he forgets the minor divisions of street and town, and calls him *countryman, i.e. countyman:* but if in their foreign excursions they should associate in France, or any other part of *Europe,* their local remembrance would be enlarged into that of *Englishmen.* And by a just parity of reasoning, all

Europeans meeting in America, or any other quarter of the globe, are *countrymen;* for England, Holland, Germany, or Sweden, when compared with the whole, stand in the same places on the larger scale, which the divisions of street, town, and county do on the smaller ones; Distinctions too limited for Continental minds. Not one third of the inhabitants, even of this province [Pennsylvania], are of English descent. Wherefore, I reprobate the phrase of Parent or Mother Country applied to England only, as being false, selfish, narrow, and ungenerous.

But, admitting that we were all of English descent, what does it amount to? Nothing. Britain, being now an open enemy, extinguishes every other name and title: and to say that reconcilation is our duty, is truly farcical. The first king of England, of the present line (William and Conqueror) was a Frenchman, and half of the peers of England are descendants from the same country; wherefore, by the same method of reasoning, England ought to be governed by France.

Much hath been said of the united strength of Britain and the Colonies, that in conjunction they might bid defiance to the world: But this is mere presumption; the fate of war is uncertain, neither do the expressions mean any thing; for this continent would never suffer itself to be drained of inhabitants, to support the British arms in either Asia, Africa, or Europe.

Besides, what have we to do with setting the world at defiance? Our plan is commerce, and that, well attended to, will secure us the peace and friendship of all Europe; because it is the interest of all Europe to have America a free port. Her trade will always be a protection, and her barrenness of gold and silver secure her from invaders.

I challenge the warmest advocate for reconciliation to show a single advantage that this continent can reap by being connected with Great Britain. I repeat the challenge, not a single advantage is derived. Our corn will fetch its price in any market in Europe, and our imported goods must be paid for, buy them where we will.

But the injuries and disadvantages which we sustain by that connection, are without number; and our duty to mankind at large, as well as to ourselves, instruct us to renounce the alliance: because, any submission to, or dependance on, Great Britain, tends directly to involve this Continent in European wars and quarrels, and set us at variance with nations who would otherwise seek our friendship, and against whom we have neither anger nor complaint. As Europe is our market for trade, we ought to form no partial connection with any part of it. It is the true interest of America to steer clear of European contentions, which she never can do, while, by her dependance on Britain, she is made the makeweight in the scale of British politics.

Europe is too thickly planted with Kingdoms to be long at peace, and whenever a war breaks out between England and any foreign power, the trade of America goes to ruin, *because of her connection with Britain.* The next war may not turn out like the last, and should it not, the advocates for reconciliation now will be wishing for separation then, because neutrality in that case would be a safer convoy than a man of war. Everything that is right or reasonable pleads for separation. The blood of the slain, the weeping voice of nature cries, 'TIS TIME TO PART. Even the distance at which the Almighty hath placed England and America is a strong and natural proof that the authority of the one over the other, was never the design of Heaven. The time likewise at which the Continent was discovered, adds weight to the argument, and the manner in which it was peopled, increases the force of it. The Reformation was preceded by the discovery of America: As if the Almighty graciously meant to open a sanctuary to the persecuted in future years, when home should afford neither friendship nor safety.

The authority of Great Britain over this continent, is a form of government which sooner or later must have an end: And a serious mind can draw no true pleasure by looking forward, under the painful and positive conviction that what he calls "the present constitution" is merely temporary. As parents, we can have no joy, knowing that this government is not sufficiently lasting to insure any thing which we may bequeath to posterity: And by a plain method of argument, as we are running the next generation into debt, we ought to do the work of it, otherwise we use them meanly and pitifully. In order to discover the line of our duty rightly, we should take our children in our hand, and fix our station a few years farther into life; that eminence will present a prospect which a few present fears and prejudices conceal from our sight.

Though I would carefully avoid giving unnecessary offence, yet I am inclined to believe that all those who espouse the doctrine of reconciliation may be included within the following descriptions.

Interested men, who are not to be trusted, weak men who *cannot* see, prejudiced men who will not see, and a certain set of moderate men who think better of the European world than it deserves; and this last class, by an ill-judged deliberation, will be the cause of more calamities to this Continent than all the other three.

It is the good fortune of many to live distant from the scene of present sorrow; the evil is not sufficiently brought to their doors to make them feel the precariousness with which all American property is possessed. But let our imaginations transport us a few moments to Boston; that seat of wretchedness will teach us wisdom, and instruct us forever to renounce a power in which we can have no trust. The inhabitants of that unfortunate city who but a few months ago were in ease and affluence, have now no other alternative than to stay and starve, or turn out to beg. Endangered by the fire of their friends if they continue within the city, and plundered by the soldiery if they leave it, in their present situation they are prisoners without the hope of redemption, and in a general attack for their relief they would be exposed to the fury of both armies.

Men of passive tempers look somewhat lightly over the offences of Great Britain, and, still hoping for the best, are apt to call out, *Come, come, we shall be friends again for all this.* But examine the passions and feelings of mankind: bring the doctrine of reconciliation to the touchstone of nature, and then tell me whether you can hereafter love, honour, and faithfully serve the power that hath carried fire and sword into your land? If you cannot do all these, then are you only deceiving yourselves, and by your delay bringing ruin upon posterity. Your future connection with Britain, whom you can neither love nor honour, will be forced and unnatural, and being formed only on the plan of present convenience, will in a little time fall into a relapse more wretched than the first. But if you say, you can still pass the violations over, then I ask, hath your house been burnt? Hath your property been destroyed before your face? Are your wife and children destitute of a bed to lie on, or bread to live on? Have you lost a parent or child by their hands, and yourself the ruined and wretched survivor? If you have not, then are you not a judge of those who have. But if you have, and can still shake hands with the murderers, then are you unworthy the name of husband, father, friend, or lover, and whatever may be your rank or title in life, you have the heart of a coward, and the spirit of a sychophant.

This is not inflaming or exaggerating matters, but trying them by those feelings and affections which nature justifies, and without which we should be incapable of discharging the social duties of life, or enjoying the felicities of it. I mean not to exhibit horror for the purpose of provoking revenge, but to awaken us from fatal and unmanly slumbers, that we may pursue determinately some fixed object. 'Tis not in the power of Britain or of Europe to conquer America, if she doth not conquer herself by delay and timidity. The present winter is worth an age if rightly employed, but if lost or neglected the whole continent will partake of the misfortune; and there is no punishment which that man doth not deserve, be he who, or what, or where he will, that may be the means of sacrificing a season so precious and useful.

'Tis repugnant to reason, to the universal order of things, to all examples from former ages, to suppose that this Continent can long remain subject to any external power. The most sanguine in Britain doth not think so. The utmost stretch of human wisdom cannot, at this time, compass a plan, short of separation, which can promise the continent even a year's security. Reconciliation is *now* a fallacious dream. Nature hath deserted the connection, and art cannot supply her place. For, as Milton wisely expresses, "never can true reconcilement grow where wounds of deadly hate have pierced so deep."

Every quiet method for peace hath been ineffectual. Our prayers have been rejected with disdain; and hath tended to convince us that nothing flatters vanity or confirms obstinacy in Kings more than repeated petitioning—and nothing hath contributed more than that very measure to make the Kings of Europe absolute. Witness Denmark and Sweden. Wherefore, since nothing but blows will do, for God's sake let us come to a final separation, and not leave the next generation to be cutting throats under the violated unmeaning names of parent and child.

To say they will never attempt it again is idle and visionary; we thought so at the repeal of the stamp act, yet a year or two undeceived us; as well may we suppose that nations which have been once defeated will never renew the quarrel.

As to government matters, 'tis not in the power of Britain to do this

IV ~ THE CRISIS OF INDEPENDENCE

continent justice: the business of it will soon be too weighty and intricate to be managed with any tolerable degree of convenience, by a power so distant from us, and so very ignorant of us; for if they cannot conquer us they cannot govern us. To be always running three or four thousand miles with a tale or a petition, waiting four or five months for an answer, which, when obtained, requires five or six more to explain it in, will in a few years be looked upon as folly and childishness. There was a time when it was proper, and there is a proper time for it to cease.

Small islands not capable of protecting themselves are the proper objects for government to take under their care; but there is something absurd, in supposing a Continent to be perpetually governed by an island. In no instance hath nature made the satellite larger than its primary planet; and as England and America, with respect to each other, reverse the common order of nature, it is evident that they belong to different systems. England to Europe: America to itself.

I am not induced by motives of pride, party, or resentment to espouse the doctrine of separation and independence; I am clearly, positively, and conscientiously persuaded that it is the true interest of this Continent to be so; that everything short of *that* is a mere patchwork, that it can afford no lasting felicity, — that it is leaving the sword to our children, and shrinking back at a time when a little more, a little further, would have rendered this Continent the glory of the earth.

As Britain hath not manifested the least inclination towards a compromise, we may be assured that no terms can be obtained worthy the acceptance of the Continent, or any ways to equal the expence of blood and treasure we have been already put to.

The object contended for, ought always to bear some just proportion to the expense. The removal of North, or the whole detestable junto, is a matter unworthy the millions we have expended. A temporary stoppage of trade was an inconvenience, which would have sufficiently ballanced the repeal of all the acts complained of, had such repeals been obtained; but if the whole continent must take up arms, if every man must be a soldier, 'tis scarcely worth our while to fight against a contemptible ministry only. Dearly, dearly do we pay for the repeal of the acts, if that is all we fight for; for, in a just estimation, 'tis as great a folly to pay a Bunker-hill price for law as for land. As I have always considered the independancy of this continent, an event which sooner or later must arrive, so from the late rapid progress of the Continent to maturity, the event cannot be far off. Wherefore, on the breaking out of hostilities, it was not worth the while to have disputed a matter which time would have finally redressed, unless we meant to be in earnest: otherwise it is like wasting an estate on a suit at law, to regulate the trespasses of a tenant whose lease is just expiring. No man was a warmer wisher for a reconciliation than myself, before the fatal nineteenth of April, 1775, but the moment the event of that day was made known, I rejected the hardened, sullen-tempered Pharaoh of England forever; and disdain the wretch, that with the pretended title of FATHER OF HIS PEOPLE can unfeelingly hear of their slaughter, and composedly sleep with their blood upon his soul.

But admitting that matters were now made up, what would be the event? I answer, the ruin of the Continent. And that for several reasons.

First. The powers of governing still remaining in the hands of the King, he will have a negative over the whole legislation of this Continent. And as he hath shown himself such an inveterate enemy to liberty, and discovered such a thirst for arbitrary power, is he, or is he not, a proper person to say to these colonies, *You shall make no laws but what I please!?* And is there any inhabitant of America so ignorant as not to know, that according to what is called the *present constitution,* this Continent can make no laws but what the king gives leave to; and is there any man so unwise as not to see, that (considering what has happened) he will suffer no law to be made here but such as suits *his* purpose? We may be as effectually enslaved by the want of laws in America, as by submitting to laws made for us in England. After matters were made up (as it is called), can there be any doubt, but the whole power of the crown will be exerted to keep this continent as low and humble as possible? Instead of going forward we shall go backward, or be perpetually quarrelling, or ridiculously petitioning. We are already greater than the King wishes us to be, and will he not hereafter endeavor to make us less? To bring the matter to one point, Is the power who is jealous of our prosperity, a proper power to govern us? Whoever says *No* to this question is an Independant for independency means no more than this, whether we shall make our own laws, or whether the King, the greatest enemy this continent hath, or can have, shall tell us, *there shall be no laws but such as I like.*

But the king, you will say, has a negative in England; the people there can make no laws without his consent. In point of right and good order, it is something very ridiculous that a youth of twenty-one (which hath often happened) shall say to several millions of people older and wiser than himself, "I forbid this or that act of yours to be law." But in this place I decline this sort of reply, though I will never cease to expose the absurdity of it, and only answer that England being the king's residence, and America not so, makes quite another case. The king's negative here is ten times more dangerous and fatal than it can be in England; for there he will scarcely refuse his consent to a bill for putting England into as strong a state of defense as possible, and in America he would never suffer such a bill to be passed.

America is only a secondary object in the system of British politics. England consults the good of this country no further than it answers her own purpose. Wherefore, her own interest leads her to suppress the growth of ours in every case which doth not promote her advantage, or in the least interferes with it. A pretty state we should soon be in under such a second hand government, considering what has happened! Men do not change from enemies to friends by the alteration of a name: And in order to show that reconciliation now is a dangerous doctrine, I affirm *that it would be policy in the King at this time to repeal the acts, for the sake of reinstating himself in the government of the provinces;* In order that HE MAY AC-COMPLISH BY CRAFT AND SUBTLETY, IN THE LONG RUN, WHAT HE CANNOT DO BY FORCE AND VIOLENCE IN THE SHORT ONE. Reconciliation and ruin are nearly related.

Secondly. That as even the best terms which we can expect to obtain can amount to no more than a temporary expedient, or a kind of government by guardianship, which can last no longer than till the Colonies come of age, so the general face and state of things in the interim will be unsettled and unpromising. Emigrants of property will not choose to come to a country whose form of government hangs but by a thread, and who is every day tottering on the brink of commotion and disturbance; and numbers of the present inhabitants would lay hold of the interval to dispose of their effects, and quit the Continent.

But the most powerful of all arguments is, that nothing but independance, *i.e.* a Continental form of government, can keep the peace of the Continent and preserve it inviolate from civil wars. I dread the event of a reconciliation with Britain now, as it is more than probable that it will be followed by a revolt some where or other, the consequences of which may be far more fatal than all malice of Britain.

Thousands are already ruined by British barbarity; (thousands more will probably suffer the same fate). Those men have other feelings than us who have nothing suffered. All they now possess is liberty; what they before enjoyed is sacrificed to its service, and having nothing more to lose they disdain submission. Besides, the general temper of the Colonies, towards a British government will be like that of a youth who is nearly out of his time; they will care very little about her: And a government which cannot preserve the peace is no government at all, and in that case we pay our money for nothing; and pray what is it that Britain can do, whose power will be wholly on paper, should a civil tumult break out the very day after reconciliation? I have heard some men say, many of whom I believe spoke without thinking, that they dreaded an independance, fearing that it would produce civil wars: It is but seldom that our first thoughts are truly correct, and that is the case here; for there is ten times more to dread from a patched up connection than from independance. I make the sufferer's case my own, and I protest, that were I driven from house and home, my property destroyed, and my circumstances ruined, that as a man, sensible of injuries, I could never relish the doctrine of reconciliation, or consider myself bound thereby. . . .

Ye that tell us of harmony and reconciliation, can ye restore to us the time that is past? Can ye give to prostitution its former innocence? neither can ye reconcile Britain and America. The last cord now is broken, the people of England are presenting addresses against us. There are injuries which nature cannot forgive; she would cease to be nature if she did. As well can the lover forgive the ravisher of his mistress, as the Continent forgive the murders of Britain. The Almighty hath implanted in us these inextinguishable feelings for good and wise purposes. They are the Guardians of his Image in our hearts. They distinguish us from the herd of common animals. The social compact would dissolve, and justice be extirpated from the earth, or have only a casual existence were we callous to the touches of affection. The robber and the murderer would often escape unpunished, did not the injuries which our tempers sustain, provoke us into justice.

O ye that love mankind! Ye that dare oppose not only the tyranny but the tyrant, stand forth! Every spot of the old world is overrun with oppression. Freedom hath been hunted round the Globe. Asia and Africa have long expelled her. Europe regards her like a stranger, and England hath given her warning to depart. O! receive the fugitive, and prepare in time an asylum for mankind.

B.

CATO

❡The most nearly effective reply to "Common Sense" was the series of articles by the Reverend William Smith, signing himself "Cato." Smith tried to deal not only with Paine but with "Cassandra," the disguise adopted by James Cannon, tutor of mathematics in Smith's own College of Philadelphia. An Anglican minister, Smith was educated in Scotland and became the first Provost (President) of what is now the University of Pennsylvania. His first article defended the Loyalist-dominated legislature of the colony, and he then proceeded in his second to meet Cannon and Paine. (Force, *American Archives*, 4 series V, 187–90, 444–46, 514–17.)]

To the People of Pennsylvania

As I propose to take my subjects as they rise out of the times, I shall leave to my next letter the further defense of our Assembly, to give room for a matter of very great importance, agreeable to what was hinted in the conclusion of my first letter.

The account which we have already received of Commissioners being appointed in *England*, and ready to embark for *America*, in order to negotiate a settlement of the present unhappy differences, has engaged the attention, and exercised the speculations of many among us. The powers with which they are to be invested, the manner in which they are to be received, how they are to be treated with, or whether they are to be treated with at all, have been canvassed agreeably to the different views or judgments of individuals.

Among others, a writer under the name of *Cassandra*, in the *Pennsylvania Evening Post* of last Saturday week, has held forth sentiments which I conceive highly disgraceful to *America*, and pernicious to society in general. He pretends to have satisfied himself (but upon what grounds I know not) that the sole view of the Administration in this commission is, to amuse and deceive — to bribe and corrupt us. And because he supposes all of us so very corruptible, he proposes, by way of prevention, to seize the Commissioners upon their first setting foot on shore, and bring them immediately, under a strong guard, to the Congress. I have too good an opinion of the virtue and good sense of my countrymen, to think they will pay any other regard to this advice than to consider the author as an enthusiast or madman.

The contest in which we are engaged is founded on the most noble and virtuous principles which can animate the mind of man. We are contending, at the risk of our lives and fortunes, against an arbitrary Ministry for the rights of *Englishmen*. The eyes of all Europe are upon us, and every generous bosom in which the pulse of liberty yet beats, sympathises with us, and is interested in our success. Our cause, therefore, being the cause of virtue, it will be expected that all our steps should be guided by it, and that, where the stock is so fair, the fruit will be proportionably perfect. Let us not disappoint these sanguine expectations by the smallest deviation from those liberal and enlarged sentiments which should mark the conduct of freemen; and, when the faithful historick page shall record the events of this glorious struggle, may not a single line in the bright annals be stained by the recital of a disgraceful action, nor future *Americans* have cause to blush for the failings of their ancestors. . . .

As we have long professed an ardent desire for peace, let us meet those who bring the terms, with that virtuous confidence which is inseparable from an upright conduct. Let us hear their proposals with patience, and consider them with candour; remembering how deeply the happiness of millions may be concerned in the issue. If what they offer be such as freemen ought to accept, my voice shall be for an immediate reconciliation, as I know of no object so worthy of a patriot as the healing our wounds, and the restoring of peace, if it has for its basis an effectual security for the liberties of *America*. If, on the contrary, the terms which may be offered should be such as we cannot accept, we have only to say so, and the negotiation will be at an end. . . .

Upon the whole, it appears that this writer is more an enemy to the business on which the Commissioners are to be sent, than really apprehensive for our virtue. He seems to have drank deep of the cup of Independence; to be inimical to whatever carries the appearance of peace; and too ready to sacrifice the happiness of a great Continent to his favourite plan. Among such writers, I pretend not to class myself; for I am bold to declare, and hope yet to make it evident to every honest man, that the true interest of *America* lies in reconciliation with *Great Britain* upon constitutional principles; and I can truly say, I wish it upon no other terms.

Why the many publications in favour of Independency (with which our presses have lately groaned) have passed hitherto unnoticed, I am not able to determine. But there are certainly times when publick affairs become so interesting, that every man becomes a debtor to the community for his opinions, either in speaking or writing. Perhaps it was thought best, where an appeal was pretended to be made to the common sense of this country, to leave the people for a while to the free exercise of that good understanding which they are known to possess. Those who made the appeal have little cause to triumph in its success. Of this they seem sensible; and, like true quacks, are constantly pestering us with their additional doses, till the stomachs of their patients begin wholly to revolt. If little notice has yet been taken of the publications concerning Independence, it is neither owing to the popularity of the doctrine, the unanswerable nature of the arguments, nor the fear of opposing them, as the vanity of the authors would suggest. I am confident that nine-tenths of the people of *Pennsylvania* yet abhor the doctrine.

If we look back to the origin of the present controversy, it will appear that some among us at least have been constantly enlarging their views, and stretching them beyond their first bounds, till at length they have wholly changed their ground. From the claim of Parliament to tax us, sprung the first resistance on our part. Before that unjust claim was set on foot, not an individual, not one of all the profound legislators with which this country abounds, ever held out the idea of Independence. We considered our connection with *Great Britain* as our chief happiness — we flourished, and grew rich and populous, to a degree not to be parallelled in history. Let us then act the part of skillful physicians, and wisely adapt the remedy to the evil. . . .

I have, in my second letter, freely declared my political creed, viz: "That the true interest of *America* lies in reconciliation with *Great Britain* upon constitutional principles, and that I wish it upon none else." I now proceed to give my reasons for this declaration. It is fit, in so great a question, that you should weigh both sides well, and exercise that good sense for which the inhabitants of these Colonies have been hitherto distinguished; and then I shall be under no apprehensions concerning the pernicious, though specious plans, which are every day published in our newspapers and pamphlets. The people generally judge right, when the whole truth is plainly laid before them; but through inattention in some, and fondness for novelty in others, when but one side of a proposition is agitated and persevered in, they may gradually deceive themselves, and adopt what cooler reflection and future dear-bought experience may prove to be ruinous.

Agriculture and commerce have hitherto been the happy employments, by which these Middle Colonies have risen into wealth and importance. By them the face of the country has been changed from a barren wilderness into the hospitable abodes of peace and plenty. Without them, we had either never existed as *Americans*, or existed only as Savages. The oaks would still have possessed their native spots of earth, and never have appeared in the form of ships and houses. What are now well cultivated fields, or flourishing cities, would have remained only the solitary haunts of wild beasts, or of men equally wild.

That much of our former felicity was owing to the protection of *England* is not to be denied; and that we might still derive great advantages from her protection and friendship, if not valued at too high a price, is equally certain; nor is it worth inquiring whether that protection was afforded us more for her own sake than ours. That the former was the case, more especially since the Colonies grew into consequence, I have not the least doubt; but that this is a reason for our rejecting any future connection with her I must utterly deny. Although I consider her as having, in her late conduct towards us, acted the part of a cruel stepdame, and not of a fostering parent; I would not therefore quarrel with the benefits I may reap from a connection with her, and can expect to reap nowhere else. If, by her fleets and armies, every nation on the globe is deterred from invading our properties, either on the high-seas, in foreign countries, or on our own coasts, ought we not, in sound policy, to profit by her strength; and, without regarding the motives of her conduct, embrace the opportunity of becoming rich and powerful in her friendship, at an expense far less than it would cost us merely to exist in alliance with any other power?

If our present differences can be accommodated, there is scarce a probability that she will ever renew the late fatal system of policy, or attempt to employ a force against us. But should she be so infatuated, at any future period, as to think of subjugating us, either by the arts of corruption or oppressive exertions of power, can we entertain a doubt but that we shall again, with a virtue equal to the present, and with the weapons of defence in our hands (when necessary) convince her that we are willing, by a constitutional connection with her, to afford and receive reciprocal benefits; but, although subjects of the same King, we will not consent to be her slaves. It was on this ground, and not for the purpose of trying new forms of Government, or erecting separate independent States, "that *America* embarked in the present glorious contest." On this ground, and upon none else, the Continental Union is formed. On this ground we have a powerful support among the true sons of liberty in *Great Britain;* and lastly, upon this ground, we have the utmost assurance of obtaining a full redress of our grievances, and an ample security against any future violation of our just rights. And if hereafter, in the fulness of time, it shall be necessary to separate from the land that gave birth to our ancestors, it will be in our state of perfect manhood, when we can fully wield our own arms, and protect our commerce and coasts by our own fleets, without looking to any nation upon earth for assistance.

This, I say, was our ground, and these our views, universally declared, from the origin of this contest till within a few weeks ago, when some gleams of reconciliation began first to break in upon us. If we now mean to change this ground, and reject all propositions of peace, from that moment we are deserted by every advocate of our cause in *Great Britain;* we falsify every declaration which the Congress hath heretofore held forth in our behalf; we abandon all prospect of preserving our importance by trade and agriculture – the ancient, sure, and experienced road to wealth and happiness.

In short, if thus contradicting all our former public professions, we should now affect Independency as our own act, before it appears clearly to the world to have been forced upon us by the cruel hand of the parent state, we could neither hope for union nor success in the attempt. We must be considered as a faithless people in the sight of mankind, and could scarcely expect the confidence of any nation upon earth, or look up to Heaven for its approving sentence. On the contrary, every convulsion attendant upon revolutions and innovations of Government, untimely attempted or finally defeated, might be our portion; added to the loss of trade for want of protection; the consequent decay of husbandry; bloodshed and desolation; with an exchange of the easy and flourishing condition of farmers and merchants, for a life, at best, of hardy poverty as soldiers or hunters.

To see *America* reduced to such a situation may be the choice of adventurers who have nothing to lose, or of men exalted by the present confusions into lucrative offices, which they can hold no longer than the continuance of the publick calamities. But can it be the wish of all that great and valuable body of people in *America*, who, by honest industry, have acquired a competency, and have experienced a happier life? Can it be their wish, I say, for such considerations, to have destruction continually before their eyes; and to have enormous debts entailed upon them and their posterity, till at length they have nothing left which they can truly call their own?

I know the answers which will be given to these questions, and am prepared to reply to them, with that temper and gravity which so serious a subject requires. It will be asserted — indeed it has already been asserted — that the animosities between *Great Britain* and the Colonies are now advanced to such a height that reconciliation is impossible. But assertions are nothing, when opposed to the nature of things, the truth of history, and all past experience. The quarrels of nations, being neither personal or private, cannot stir up mutual hatred among individuals. There never was a war so implacable, even among States naturally rivals and enemies, or among savages themselves, as not to have peace for its object as well as end. And among people naturally friends, and connected by every dearer tie, who knows not that their quarrels (as those of lovers) are often but a stronger renewal of love? In such cases, the tide of affection, reverting to its course, is like that of water long pent back, which, at length bursting the opposing mounds, breaks forward through its native channel, and flows with redoubled vigour and increased velocity, to mix itself with its parent main. . . .

One side of a great question has been held up to us. We are told that it can never be our interest to have any future connection with *Great Britain*, and are pressed immediately to declare our total separation; for now is the time, and the time has found us. Could it be expected that all *America* would instantly take a leap in the dark? or that any who had not a predilection for the doctrine, or were capable of reasoning upon it, would swallow it in the gross, without wishing to hear the arguments on the other side? I am sure this is the wish of multitudes of good men — particularly of those who may be principally concerned in deciding the question, and whose earnest desire it is not only to know the sense of individuals, but the clear sense of their country upon it; without which, they could not think themselves at liberty to give their decision.

Upon this ground, then, I proceed, and shall rest the cause with my adversaries on the present general defence, which (although I am sorry it was necessary) I have reason to think will be more acceptable to the publick than the misspending time in private altercation. Those who oppose me may enjoy, for a while, (perhaps unnoticed,) all the triumph of the answers they may give; and if it is found at last, as has been already hinted, that I have said nothing to the purpose, their side of the question will only be strengthened.

In my remarks upon the pamphlet before me, I shall first consider those arguments on which the author appears to lay his chief stress; and these are collected under four heads, in his conclusion:

"It is the custom of nations, when any two are at war, for some other Powers, not engaged in the quarrel, to step in as mediators, and bring about the preliminaries of peace. But while *America* calls herself a subject of *Great Britain*, no Power, however well disposed she may be, can offer her mediation."

Is this *common sense* or common nonsense? Surely peace with *Great*

Britain cannot be the object of this writer, after the horrible character he has given us of the people of that country, and telling us that reconciliation with them would be ruin. The latter part of the paragraph seems to cast some light upon the former, although it contradicts it; for these mediators are not to interfere for making up the quarrel, but to widen it, by supporting us in a declaration that we are not subjects of *Great Britain*. A new sort of business, truly, for mediators!

But this leads us directly to the main inquiry, What foreign Powers are able to give us this support? Whether they can be persuaded to engage with us? What will be their terms? Is an alliance with them safe; or is it to be preferred to an honourable and firm renewal of that ancient connection under which we have so long flourished? . . . [The author argues that we cannot count on aid from those who have always been our enemies, and who were opposed to the independence of colonies because they had colonies of their own; who furthermore were Catholic powers, and might end by conquering America for their own dominion.]

In short, I am not able, with all the pains I have taken, to understand what is meant by a Declaration of Independence; unless it is to be drawn up in the form of a solemn abjuration of Great Britain, as a nation with which we can never more be connected. And this seems the doctrine of the author of *Common Sense*. But I believe he has made but a few converts to this part of his scheme; for who knows to what vicissitudes of fortune we may yet be subjected?

We have already declared ourselves independent, as to all useful purposes, by resisting our oppressors upon our own foundation. And while we keep upon this ground, without connecting ourselves with any foreign nations, to involve us in fresh difficulties, and endanger our liberties still further, we are able, in our own element, (upon the shore,) to continue this resistance; and it is our duty to continue it, till *Great Britain* is convinced (as she must soon be) of her fatal policy, and open her arms to reconciliation, upon the permanent and sure footing of mutual interest and safety.

Upon such a footing, we may again be happy. Our trade will be revived. Our husbandmen, our mechanicks, our artificers, will flourish. Our language, our laws, and manners, being the same with those of the nation with which we are again to be connected, that connection will be natural; and we shall the more easily guard against future innovations. *Pennsylvania* has much to lose in this contest, and much to hope from a proper settlement of it. We have long flourished under our Charter Government. What may be the consequences of another form we cannot pronounce with certainty; but this we know, that it is a road we have not travelled, and may be worse than it is described.

CATO.

[The early decision for independence meant success for the Hopkinsons and Paines, failure for Leonard, Seabury, and Smith. The arguments of the Loyalists had not prevailed. Why was this so? Did they have, in reality, a superior case, and was the victory of the radicals due to factors other than men's reason or morality? The Loyalists no doubt would have inisted that their countrymen had indeed been swayed by the irrational and the evil passions. Yet it may be that the Tory words reveal the Tory mind unsuited to the crisis. Perhaps it was they who did not measure up to the times. Two final questions demand an answer: who was right; and why — regardless of right — did the rebels succeed in obtaining first a vigorous opposition to British measures, and finally independence?]

FOR FURTHER READING

There is no really first-rate book covering the whole Revolutionary period. The most readable recent survey is John C. Miller, *Origins of the American Revolution* (Boston: Little, 1943; Stanford: Stanford Univ. Press, 1959). For background, Clinton Rossiter, *Seedtime of the Republic* (New York: Harcourt, 1953) is excellent. A fine brief treatment of the reasons for independence is Carl Becker, *The Eve of the Revolution* (New Haven: Yale Univ. Press, 1921). Arthur M. Schlesinger has written an entertaining and informative account of the press's role in *Prelude to Independence: The Newspaper War on Britain, 1764–1776* (New York: Knopf, 1958). An understanding of loyalism can best be gained through Leonard Woods Labaree, *Conservatism in Early American History* (New York: New York Univ. Press, 1948; Ithaca: Cornell Univ. Press, 1959), especially in the last chapter and, most of all, through his article "The Nature of American Loyalism," American Antiquarian Society, *Proceedings,* new series, LIV (1944).